NURSES

Who Led the Way

By ADELE and
   CATEAU DE LEEUW

Illustrated by KATHERINE SAMPSON

WHITMAN PUBLISHING COMPANY

RACINE, WISCONSIN

CONTENTS

Cyclone in Calico

MARY ANN BICKERDYKE

Young Dr. Woodward stopped his horse and buggy in front of three tents. "This is my hospital," he said.

Mary Ann Bickerdyke refused his hand and stepped down into the thick mud, clutching her carryall with the precious supplies in it. Her gray calico dress was plain and serviceable; her keen blue eyes, shaded under the black cotton Shaker bonnet, saw everything. There was work to be done here, and she was dressed for working.

"Don't stand there," she told him impatiently. "Show me what's to be seen so I can start."

She was here because of a letter he had written to his pastor, Dr. Beecher, back in Galesburg, Illinois. But he did not want her here. The general did not approve of women at army encampments; Dr. Woodward hoped she would not stay long.

Mrs. Bickerdyke followed him into the tents. It was much worse than his letter had said. Ten men were crowded into one tent, lying mostly on straw pallets on the filthy mud floor with only an army blanket or winter coat over them. There was no room between the pallets. The air was thick with unpleasant smells; bluebottle flies buzzed around the patients. The water bucket was empty. It was the same, or worse, in all the tents.

"Get me some men," she ordered the doctor.

He said, "I can't—I'm only a junior medical officer."

She snorted, and marched over to the nearest campfire where the men were eating their meal of half-raw salt pork, boiled beans, and hardtack.

"How'd you like some fried chicken and some light bread with blackberry jam?" she asked in her hearty voice. The men stared at her, unbelieving. "The doctor and I've got a job to be done. We need strong fellows to help. If you help us I can find you some better grub than this!"

They leaped up, half a dozen of them. Mrs. Bickerdyke issued her orders. There were no tubs, so she had men saw casks in two. Water was boiled in every container she could find. She opened her carryall and brought out cakes of strong laundry soap. Then she went into the first tent.

"You men want a bath and a clean bed and some good supper? Then those of you who can walk, walk out of here and get scrubbed up. Those who can't we'll carry. . . . Doctor, you boss this job. Got some scissors on you? Then cut off their whiskers . . . I can see graybugs from here. New drawers and undershirts is in them carryalls. Burn all their old clothes . . . and the straw and blankets, too. And get me some clean straw."

The doctor was horrified. He was not used to being ordered about like this. And besides, he said, some of these men had high fevers. It would kill them to be taken out-of-doors and bathed.

"Fiddle-faddle!" said Mrs. Bickerdyke. "Not a breath of air stirring, and it's ninety in the shade. Won't kill any of 'em. . . . Get them clothes off, sonny," she said to the first man.

While the volunteers helped the ill men bathe, she tucked up her calico skirts and went inside the filthy tent with a spade. She and a young man named Andy Somerville scraped and shoveled until the place was fairly clean. Andy admired her. "You sound like my ma," he said.

She ruffled his hair. "You're a good lad. Go on now and clean up the other tents the way we done this. And don't forget there'll be fried chicken at the end of this."

By late afternoon the men were bathed and back in bed, resting on clean sheets spread over the clean straw. Then she got out the hampers of food she had brought from Galesburg and fed them. The grateful men followed her with their eyes.

Dr. Woodward was worried. "The sunset gun will sound soon, ma'am . . . you'd better go. You've got to be out of here by sundown."

"Nonsense," said Mary Bickerdyke. "I got to see about them pails of water first." And she did.

She told the men what she expected of them —that she had cleaned the tents and expected them to be kept that way. The doctor tried to get her to hurry; she would miss her train back to Galesburg.

She rolled down her sleeves. "Think I was leaving here?" she asked. "There's plenty more to do. I've just begun. I'll be back tomorrow and I'll stay as long as I'm needed. Don't you worry, Doctor. You needn't come with me. I'll get myself a room in town . . . and I can walk if need be."

Andy Somerville called out. "Good night, Mother!"

"Goodnight, son," she said and set off down the road. "See you in the morning."

In the years to come, countless men in the service were to call her Mother. Mother Bickerdyke, whose sole concern was the care and comfort of her "boys."

She had two boys of her own. Her husband was dead and she supported herself by doing practical nursing in Galesburg, a comfortable college town to which she had moved some years before. The townsfolk honored her as a hardworking, respectable woman who knew a great deal about herbs and "botanic medicine," which she had studied with a Dr. Hussey. She believed, ahead of her times, in cleanliness and rest and air and water and the simple herbal remedies, and most of her patients got well sooner than those who were cared for by doctors.

She had been in church that Sunday morning when Dr. Beecher read the moving letter from young Dr. Woodward at his post in the Army encampment at Cairo, Illinois. Dr. Beecher called for volunteers to collect money and supplies, and five hundred dollars' worth was subscribed in short order. Then he asked for someone to take the supplies to Cairo and see that they were properly distributed. For one reason or another no man could go. And then someone got up and said, "Why not a woman? A woman's what they need down there—a woman with a big heart and one who knows how to care for them. And who knows better than Mary Ann Bickerdyke?"

Their eyes turned to where she sat, quiet and concerned, at the back of the church with her two young sons. She thought a moment and then she said, "I'm no hand at speech-making. You give me a job to do and I gather it's a hard one. I'm used to hard jobs. All I ask is that some of you look after my boys here. Once I get them off my mind you don't need to worry. I'll go to Cairo and I'll clean things up down there. The generals and all ain't going to stop me. This is the Lord's work you're calling me to do. When I'm doing the Lord's work, they ain't nobody big enough to stop me."

Nobody stopped Mary Ann Bickerdyke from then on, although a good many people tried to at various times.

When the Civil War began, there was a great deal of confusion in Army circles. It had been a long time since the country had fought a major war. How many men would they need? How many supplies? How would they be transported? How would the wounded be cared for?

There was no American Red Cross, but, after a time, a Sanitary Commission was organized by Dr. Henry Bellows, a Unitarian clergyman, who had seen how the British Sanitary Commission worked and had gone to the Army Medical Department and proposed a similar organization. The Commission, he said, would advise on camp locations, water supply, and control of contagious diseases. It would send its own inspectors to see whether regulations were obeyed, and these inspectors would be civilians.

Dr. Bellows had a hard time convincing the Army of his plan, but finally it was accepted. The Army said the Commission could act as advisors only and would have no power to enforce the things it recommended.

Hospitals were in a dreadful condition, as the inspectors found out. The soldiers were afraid to go to them, preferring to be taken care of in army camps or to die on the field. "We need beds and bedding, hospital clothing and sick-diet, proper medicines, surgical instruments, and good nurses," wrote a soldier when the war was already eight months old. It was two years before the Army Medical Department was able to supply these things in any quantity, and even then the supplies were often held up for lack of transportation.

For those two years the Sanitary Commission

was the main supplier of the Army's hospital needs, furnishing everything from crutches to specially equipped trains and steamboats. The money came from voluntary donations in cash and in goods, and it became one of Mary Ann Bickerdyke's main jobs to see that money was sent rather than home-packed boxes of goodies which rotted or fermented on the railroad sidings. When supplies did come in, she commandeered them for her boys. The well soldiers could live on army fare, she said, but nothing was too good for her boys—so when she found what she wanted in railroad cars she ordered it delivered to her hospital and prepared it for her invalids.

She found on her second day in Cairo that Dr. Woodward's hospital was only one of six, two of them across the river. The others were in worse condition than the first she had seen. She scoured and cleaned and demanded fresh supplies until the patients cheered her and the doctors found her a great nuisance.

She did not hesitate to tell them what she thought of them, and one doctor was so enraged he went straight to headquarters.

"That woman—that woman," he cried, "is a cyclone in calico!"

The general was sure he could deal with the matter. He sent for Dr. Woodward and Mrs. Bickerdyke. No one knows exactly what took place in the interview, but afterward Mother Bickerdyke said simply, "I talked sense into him."

Another general, U. S. Grant, became her

stanch friend and supporter. After he took the Confederate Fort Donelson in one of the hardest-fought battles of the war, Mother Bickerdyke was on the hospital ship that went from Cairo to remove the wounded. No one knows how she got aboard, but there she was—running the kitchen, taking care of the wounded, supplying fresh linen, washing the blood-caked uniforms, making up the beds. She was everywhere at once. One of the volunteer surgeons aboard said, "I never saw anyone like her!"

Five times the hospital ship came to take away the wounded. Mother Bickerdyke was not satisfied that everyone had been removed from the battle-field, and late at night she went out with her lantern, moving slowly over the frozen ground, to search for one more living "boy." When one of the patients asked her, "Aren't you tired, Mother Bickerdyke?" she answered, "What if I am? I'm well and strong, and I want you to be, too."

It is small wonder that when they saw her the

soldiers cheered her, three times three, with deaf-
ening hurrahs. They came to know her answer to
that. "For heaven's sake, stop your nonsense,
boys," she would say, "and shut up!"

When she was appointed an agent of the
Sanitary Commission, she brought down endless
worries on the Commission's heads, for she
blandly ordered what she needed whether the
Commission had funds to pay for things or not.
She needed supplies, she said, and it was up to
them to find ways to pay for them. The Commission finally discovered that if they made a public
appeal in the name of Mother Bickerdyke, the
money rolled in.

She went with the Army to Savannah, Tennessee, to nurse the troops, and while there the
dreadful Battle of Shiloh took place. It was a surprise attack and countless men were wounded.
Mother Bickerdyke was tireless, distributing
stores of condensed food, clothing, stimulants,
chloroform, and surgical instruments. When the

Commission's ships did not bring sufficient supplies, she drove about the countryside in a buggy
foraging for eggs, milk, butter, and fowl.

She called the Secessionists the "secesh" and
was not above taking what she required from
them without their leave. But when a Southern
boy was brought in with a serious wound, he
received the same gentle, loving care that her
Northern boys did. There she could see no difference.

Her calico dresses often caught fire as she
tended her cooking over the logs in the open air,
and soldiers were forever rescuing her. The state
of her clothing became known and wealthy
women from the North sent down bundles of fine
dresses. She had no intention of wearing them
herself, but she used them in trade for fruit and
honey for her soldiers. Someone sent her two
beautiful nightgowns trimmed with ruffles and
lace. "Nothing like that for me!" she snorted, but
she put them in her bag and had them with her

when she came upon an ambulance standing on a railroad track.

Inside were two hungry, dirty soldiers going home on furlough, their undressed wounds swarming with vermin. Mother Bickerdyke cleaned their wounds and then hunted for bandages. There were none.

"Now I see why the good Lord sent them furbelowed nightgowns!" she cried and tore the bottoms off in strips to make her bandages. Then she made the men wear the nightgowns instead of their blood-soaked shirts. At first they held out against her, but no one withstood Mother Bickerdyke for long. The men wore them to their destination and refused to exchange them for hospital shirts. A quarter of a century later one of them was found preserved as a precious war relic in a Wisconsin home.

It was two years before Mother Bickerdyke, exhausted from her duties, had her first furlough. She went to visit her good friend Mrs. Livermore, in Chicago, and while there she attended a wedding. The handsome young bridegroom rushed up to her when he saw her. "Mother Bickerdyke! Remember me? Because of you I'm here today."

"I don't quite remember, son—"

"It was after Donelson. I had a Minie ball in my leg, and they wanted to amputate, but you wouldn't let them, and you saved it!"

She was as happy about it as he, but so many thousand cases had been ministered to by her hands. The wedding guests wanted to hear more; long after the bride and groom had departed they stayed on to hear her stories of the war, the hospitals, and the camps. Mrs. Livermore realized what a priceless gift her guest had for reaching the hearts of hearers, and she made Mrs. Bickerdyke promise to visit various cities before she went back on duty, to tell people of what she had seen firsthand. As a result, her moved hearers pledged money for supplies and medicine—and that's how she spent her first vacation!

There were ten thousand military patients in the Memphis hospitals when Mary Ann Bickerdyke reported there for duty. The young doctor in charge resented Mother Bickerdyke's independence and did not like her grammar. When he found she had employed more than fifty Negroes, who were known as *contrabands,* to help her, he ordered them to leave.

Mother Bickerdyke heard of the order. It was late at night, but there was no time to lose. She got in her ambulance, drove over the rough, dark roads, found the general, routed him out of bed, and would not leave until he had signed a paper. Next morning, when the young doctor came into her kitchen and found the Negro helpers still there, he was furious. "You'll leave here before you're a week older!" he stormed.

Mother Bickerdyke laid down her spoon and advanced upon him. "I'll not leave!" she cried. "I've enlisted for this war, as these boys have, and I'll not go home before them! And, Doctor, you'd

better not get into a row with me. When anybody does, one of us two always goes to the wall, and 'tain't never me!"

Something about her—her voice, her words, the fire in her eye—made him realize what a challenge she had thrown him. Instead of sending her away, he became her friend and continued to be one of her best friends and helpers.

She could be all tenderness when she was feeding one of her boys or bathing his wounds, but that "fire in her eye" was present when she found neglect or injustice. A young surgeon came in one morning, yawning, after spending the night in town instead of attending to his wounded. She stood up and commanded, "Off with your shoulder straps and get out of this hospital!"

The surgeon complained to General Sherman himself, and Sherman asked, "Who is your accuser?"

When he heard it was Mother Bickerdyke, he said with a smile, "I'm afraid I can't help you. She ranks me. There is nothing left for you to do except to carry your case before President Lincoln."

Mother Bickerdyke was not downed by difficulties. When she was unable to get milk and eggs of the quality she desired in Memphis and was told that they could not be sent from the North because they would spoil en route, she sniffed. "Hm, eggs come from hens, don't they? And milk from cows?"

She went north and told one of the wealthy

farmers of Illinois, "I want cows." He gave her some from his own herds and persuaded his neighbors to do likewise. Then she called for chickens. When she went south again she took with her more than a hundred cows and a thousand chickens. People in Memphis couldn't stand the noise, so the "farm" was moved to an island outside the city. Here she arranged her dairy and hennery, and her boys had their fresh milk and eggs.

The following year, she was in charge of the field hospital near Chattanooga, after the bloody battle of Lookout Mountain. Army wagons couldn't haul supplies fast enough, and men and mules were starving. Mother Bickerdyke found an abandoned mill with a great quantity of flour that had belonged to the Confederates. She baked bread in brick ovens which she had set up from demolished chimneys. But there wasn't enough, and another abandoned mill could not be located.

On the last day of the year it was so cold that the thermometers broke. Men had only summer uniforms; wind was of hurricane force, rain turned to ice. Hospital tents were overturned, the sick soldiers rolled to the ground. Wounds re-opened, bones that had been set were fractured again.

The log fires burned high, but in the middle of the night the flames died down, and there were no more logs. It was impossible to cut trees in the frozen forest. The officer in charge was in despair.

"We must try to pull through," he said. "Good night."

But Mother Bickerdyke could not let her boys freeze. She thought hard and fast. She made panado—a mixture of crackers, sugar, hot water, and whisky—and took it to her soldiers. Then, looking at the piled logs of the breastworks she had a sudden idea. They could burn the logs from the breastworks!

She had no permission to do such a thing, but the Pioneer Corps decided it could not refuse her orders, either, and willing hands pulled down the logs with axes, hooks, and chains. Soon the logs burned again, and Mother ran from tent to tent, carrying hot drinks and hot bricks.

In the midst of her work thirteen more ambulances arrived with men who had been on the way all day and were delayed by the storm. Their bandages were glass, their feet were frozen, their hands were like marble. The surgeon amputated all through the night, and Mother Bickerdyke did her wonderful best to comfort the dying, to save the living, and to bring comfort to all of them, as she could.

In the morning when the commandant of the post found the demolished breastworks he cried, "Madam, consider yourself under arrest!" But Mother Bickerdyke, a can of panado in one hand, a hot brick in the other, brushed him aside. "All right, I'm under arrest. Only don't meddle with me now, or my men will freeze to death." And she would not stop.

When the court inquiry took place, Mother

Bickerdyke gave them a piece of her mind to such good effect that an officer whispered in her ear, "Pursue the same course again under the same circumstances." Mother Bickerdyke was free to continue her work.

Wherever the Army fought, there was Mary Ann Bickerdyke. General Sherman gave her a pass that permitted her to go back and forth across the lines, and she made good use of it. On several occasions she was the only woman with thousands of men, and everywhere men revered her and loved her salty speech and her kind smile and her deft hands. She was in all the worst places; in pesthouses and under fire and at the dreadful prison of Andersonville.

When the war ended, there was still work for her. She managed a home for soldiers, and one for children; she traveled the country over, searching out men who needed pensions and working for them in Washington. Her grown sons begged her to come and live with them and take it easy, and she did for a while . . . but there was always something new for her to do, and she could not rest.

A generation after the war, men would hobble up to her or wave their crutches when she appeared. "Mother, do you remember me?" "Mother, do you remember how you found me after the siege of Vicksburg?"

Her brown hair turned gray, her deft hands became crippled; she did not have the strength now that had seen her through desperate and dreadful years of service. But to the very end she was alert and interested, doing what she could to help her "boys." Her sons made her life pleasant; the Government granted her a pension, after much trouble, of twenty-five dollars a month. A statue to her stands in Galesburg; a victory ship was named for her. But her true immortality remains in the glorious example she set of what one woman, dedicated in mind and heart, can do when she tries.

A Challenge
Worth Meeting

ANNE PROCHAZKA

A small, trim nurse climbed the dirty stairway to the upper floor and knocked on a scarred door. When there was no answer she knocked again and then entered. It was so dark inside that at first she could barely make out the mother lying in bed. The woman turned her face to her visitor and grunted.

"I'm Anne Prochazka," the nurse said, taking

33

off her gloves and setting down her bag. "They told me you were ill and needed help, and I've come to make you well if I can."

The woman looked grateful but said nothing. Anne set to work, tying on her apron, laying out her materials. It was when she looked around to see if there was a water faucet anywhere that she found the child.

She was tiny and dirty and sat hunched up on a broken-down chair in the corner. She had not uttered a sound. Her lowered head and matted hair made her look like a little animal. Her dress was filthy and torn and her bare legs dangled under the short skirt. It was the sight of those legs that made Anne Prochazka wince, although her face showed nothing of what she felt. For only one leg was normal; the other was half its right size and the little stump of a baby foot dangled halfway between knee and ground and was encased in a steel brace.

The child watched her silently, her face set in

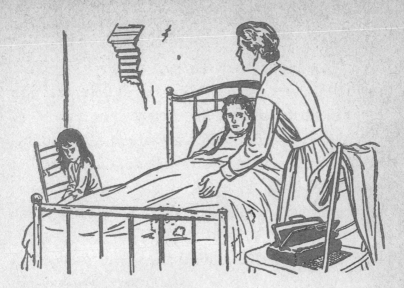

a scowl that did not lighten.

Anne said in a friendly voice, "Hello. What's your name?"

"Her name—Mary," the mother answered. Mary said nothing; the scowl deepened.

"She no walk; she jus' sit . . . all day, like this." The mother sighed. "She no like anyt'ing—no keeds, no food, nothing. All day sit . . . I go to work, she sit; I come home, she still sit."

Anne Prochazka's heart swelled with pity—and with determination. Here was a young person desperately in need of help, greater help than the mother. But she must help the mother first, and then the child. For the mother would soon get over her fever and be up and about again, but for the child it would be a long, hard pull.

Each time she came to bathe and look after the mother, Anne said, "I'd like to help Mary. She should have her stump cut off—"

"No, no!" the mother cried, and little Mary shrank up against the wall. "Not cut—never!"

"Yes, cut," Anne said firmly. "Then the doctors can put on a new leg, just the right length, and I could make the muscles work and after a while Mary would walk—like other girls."

"Not cut—not ever!" the mother said, and Mary shook her head, too.

When the mother was well, Anne said, "Now as a treat, will you let me take Mary to the Spalding School? There are so many little girls and boys her age there, I think she would like it—just for a visit."

"Okay . . . you take her," Mary's mother said. Mary said nothing, but Anne thought she saw a gleam of interest in the sullen eyes under the matted hair.

Anne had worked at the Spalding School before she had become a visiting nurse. She remembered her first day there, when she had been wondering if this would be work she liked. She stood in the hallway as the children gathered for assembly . . . Boy Scouts, some of them wearing braces, some hopping on crutches. Others being pushed in wheel chairs by Scouts who had good legs but a bad arm. Their spirit lifted her heart, and she knew she would enjoy her work. But in her days there she had come to realize that you could only help people who wanted to help themselves, and that was why she wanted to take Mary to the school. Mary would have to want to be like other children.

She called for Mary the first morning. Mary hung back, pulling on her arm, but Anne took her firmly along. At the school Mary shrank against the wall, looking at these other children who were handicapped, too, but different. They were clean, they were laughing, they were trying to walk, they were learning.

A little girl came up to her, eyes radiant. "Look!" she cried. "I've got a new leg—I just got it—but already I can walk!" And she hobbled off a few steps and back, stumbling a little, but keeping upright. Her face flushed with pride. "I can walk! Maybe next week I can run."

"Maybe not next week," Anne Prochazka said gently. "But soon, my dear. Soon."

Mary said, after a while, "*I* want to walk like that, too."

Anne's heart leaped! She tried not to show how much this meant to her. For it was the first thing Mary had said that was hopeful, that was something they could build on. Mary looked down at her withered stump and then up at Anne's face. "So—tell them they can cut it off. I don't care!

You're sure I can walk someday?"

Anne hugged the small body to her side. "Yes, I'm sure," she said. "Now let's go and tell Mother what you've decided." She stooped down and gazed into the dirty little face. "You must tell Mother how much you want this, and you must make her see it. Make her see what you saw here at the school. Then, if you want it enough and she sees how much you want it, she will let the surgeon make you well."

Mary nodded. "I—guess I can," she said. She could hardly bear to leave the busy room where the handicapped children were playing—as if they were not handicapped—and Anne Prochazka knew that Mary was imprinting that scene on her mind so that it would be strong and lasting. Mary knew she wanted to be well; she must have the strength to make her mother want it for her, too.

It wasn't too hard to make Mary's mother agree. When she realized how much her child longed to be as other children now, she realized, too, that it was what she herself had hoped for all along. Anne Prochazka explained gently what the surgeon would do, how long Mary might have to stay in the hospital while the wound healed, how the new leg would be measured and fitted to the healed stump, and then how she herself would work, day after day, to bring the muscles above the stump into use again. They followed her words, the movements of her fine hands, with eagerness, wanting to believe, wanting to be reassured, wanting to be made strong.

Mary was brave, and even her mother managed to smile on the day she went to the operating room, keeping her fears to herself. The operation, performed by a skilled surgeon, was a success, but then came the long months of healing, and Anne called on all her powers to help Mary get over that period. This was the thing she enjoyed most, this was what she had been trained for, this was the work she most wanted to do.

It was more weary months before the muscles

were educated to take up their work and before
Mary could be trained to use them with her new
artificial leg. She was as proud of her new leg as
if she had made it herself. It was opening a whole
new world for her, the world where children like
herself could walk and run and play.

On Mary's last trip to the orthopedic center
Miss Prochazka gazed at her with admiration.
"You look like a different girl," she said. "The
kind of girl I knew you could be when I first saw
you. Good luck now, Mary, and happy days!"

Mary held her hand in speechless love. She was
silent again, but it was a warm silence now.

Miss Prochazka, in her busy round, lost sight
of Mary for a good many months. There were so
many other cases she had to look out for and
work over. Then one day she met a young girl on
the street. She looked somewhat familiar, and
Anne Prochazka stole a second glance. It couldn't
be—yes, it was—*could* it be Mary? Her hair was
soft and clean and curled. It framed her piquant

face and big eyes and made her really beautiful. Mary had on a pretty dress, starched and clean, and she half ran, half skipped across the street— like any other child. Mary did not see her, and Miss Prochazka did not call out to her. She thought, *This is my reward. I've helped to make her as much like other children as possible. This is the way I shall remember her.*

She had never had any doubts about wanting to be a nurse. It was experiences such as this, however, that warmed her heart and made her strong for whatever lay ahead. *Surely,* she said to herself, *there is no other profession that gives as much to the one who serves it.* She hurried on her round with a gay smile and a song in her heart, and as she went she saw her own life and the events that had brought her to this happy moment.

When she had come to Chicago, years before, she did not speak English. She was nineteen and wanted to enter training school to be a nurse, but she had never had more than a grammar school education, and to enter training she had to have a high school diploma.

She was fourteen when she had left her native Czechoslovakia to come to America. Her father was a small-town merchant with four daughters and one son. There was not money to educate them all, but they believed in education and wanted it. Anne's oldest sister came to America first and found work as a governess in Oklahoma. Then an aunt and uncle went to Oklahoma, purchased a farm, and invited one of Anne's other sisters to live with them. At the last moment the sister fell in love and married and stayed home, so Anne had the chance to use her sister's ticket and accepted joyfully.

Traveling across America to her new home in Oklahoma she was awe-struck by the size of the country to which she had come. But she thought longingly of the beautiful mountains of her native Czechoslovakia. Life on the farm was a busy one; there was plenty of work for a fifteen-year-old girl and she tried to be as useful as possible.

At sixteen, she felt she ought to make her own way and went to Cleveland to take a housemaid's job. There wasn't much money, but she was living among her own kind of people, speaking her own language, and she was happy. The following year there were three Prochazka sisters in America; they rented a small apartment together, got jobs in a rubber-goods factory, and made a pleasant life for themselves, feeling free and independent. When she had managed to save fifty dollars she decided to make a break and get on with her ambition to become a nurse. One sister was now living in Chicago and Anne made up her mind to go there for her training. She had no idea how long it would take her to achieve her goal.

"You must have a high school diploma to enter training," they told her.

"Very well, then," she said, "I'll go to high school."

But even entering high school was not easy, for

her English was so rudimentary. "If you can write a little essay telling us how much you want to do this, we'll see what happens next," the authorities said.

Anne never worked harder at anything in her life than she worked over that paper, biting her pen, trying to summon the right words to put down, trying to make her intense feeling come through onto the bare white paper in front of her.

And it worked! The teachers saw in her face, and could read in her words, how much this meant to her, and they gave her the chance. She was nineteen to the other pupils' fourteen . . . a young woman who had already had a full life, who had earned her living and had her own apartment. She studied hard. She got herself a job in the household of a kind family where, in return for minor duties, she was assured of a home and fifty cents a week spending money. This was increased to two dollars after a short time, and Anne felt that her financial problems were solved. When, after

four happy years, she held her hard-won diploma in her hand, she was the proudest girl in the class. No one else knew what it had meant to earn it.

Her three years at the Cook County Hospital Nurses' Training School were busy ones. In that time she made her decision: She wanted to be a visiting nurse, and with the proud R.N. after her name, she applied to the Visiting Nurse Association of Chicago for a job. They put her name down but told her that while she waited she ought to have some more experience; she should do bedside nursing in people's homes before doing public health work.

She put herself on call—and on each of her first three assignments her patient died. It was a bitter blow to her and, as she said later, it made her realize that girls should not go into nursing at too young an age, for this sort of experience was hard to take. She begged then to be sent to a patient who was not going to die, for she needed the experience of helping a person get well, of making a family happy.

Fortunately for her, the Visiting Nurse Association sent for her soon thereafter and she was very happy to get placed so quickly in the work she most wanted to do. She was twenty-seven now. It had taken her nine years to reach her goal.

But Anne Prochazka did not stop there. Her work was in a poor district of the great city where disease was rampant, where children were without the proper care and food, so that often they were dull and apathetic. It was her job, as she went about, to look for other people who needed nursing care, and she looked for them not only in the homes but on the streets. She cared for newborn babies, she brought bedside care to the old and to the very ill. All the while she kept her eyes and ears open for other cases which these people might tell her about or that she saw for herself. And as she nursed them she told her patients about health matters and assisted them in their troubles. This was work she thoroughly enjoyed, and when her superiors told her she would be transferred to their orthopedic division she wasn't at all sure that she would like it.

But her first assignment in this division was at the Spalding School for crippled children. Here was a challenge worth meeting. She knew that many of the badly handicapped soldiers of the first World War had been taught to get about, to earn their livings, to enjoy life quite normally, and it was this sort of thing that she could teach the crippled children.

But she learned, too, that unless her young patients really wanted to get well, and to work with their nurse, there was little she could do with her skillful hands. She must make them *want* to learn to use their new legs and arms, she must make them *want* to exercise their feeble muscles. To do that, she herself must know all the techniques that had been developed. She was given a scholarship from the Visiting Nurse Association to go to an eight-weeks' course in physiotherapy at Harvard Medical School, and the next year she repeated the work at the famous Robert Breck Brigham Hospital in Boston. Now she had the knowledge to use wisely light, heat, water, electricity, and massage; she knew how to manipulate joints, how to give corrective exercises with her hands and with pulleys and bicycles and other apparatus.

Her superiors saw that she had a special skill for working with the crippled. She knew how to use her hands and all the latest devices, but most important of all, she knew how to approach her patients—the weary, the sick, the afraid—and give them courage and the will power to go through with the long and tedious course.

Anne Prochazka had found herself, her life work. And every time she met and helped someone like little Mary, she knew once again the joy and satisfaction of being in a profession that gave her such a tremendous reward.

More Than Patriotism

EDITH CAVELL

The young probationer climbed the stairs of the dark hospital and knocked softly on the door of the directress's room. It was chilly in the misty four o'clock dawn, and she shivered, partly from cold and partly from excitement.

Edith Cavell's voice called, "Enter!"

The probationer went in. "Here is the package, madame." She knew it contained slices of bread and some milk. Edith Cavell was ready and dressed, her blue cloak and severe black hat melting into the dimness of the austere little room. Only the fine-drawn white face stood out, composed and calm as always.

"Thank you, Pauline," she said.

There were a hundred questions Pauline wanted to ask, but she knew better. She turned and left, going back to her duties in the crowded hospital, but through the hours she waited, breathlessly.

She realized now what was happening at the Institute Depage. Only last week she had been going down the cellar steps at dawn for her refresher of bread and tea, and a shape had moved silently out of the shadows.

"It's a ghost!" she had gasped.

But the shape said comfortingly, "Hallo, nursie!" It was one of the two Englishmen Miss Cavell had taken in—a wounded colonel and a sergeant major. They had been brought to the hospital and hidden. Now they were well enough and Miss Cavell was taking them to safety.

Pauline heard the men moving almost silently down the stairs and across the hall, but Miss Cavell moved so quietly she did not even hear her. Then the front door closed and they were lost in the misty dawn.

It was three hours before Madame returned.

Pauline searched the beloved face as the nurses congregated for breakfast. Edith Cavell's deep-set eyes were calm. Pauline thought, *She has done what she set out to do!* The men were on their way to safety.

Breakfasts were meager in war-torn Brussels in 1914. The Germans occupied the city. Cannon boomed in the distance, and at night the skies were red with flames. Meat had almost disappeared from the markets; people lived on bread, fish, salads, and thin carrot soup, and there was never enough. There was never enough coal, either, and rooms were chilly and uncomfortable. But work went on, and the probationers and nurses whom Edith Cavell had trained in this small hospital, set up and run by the brilliant Dr. Henri Depage, were devoted to her and did not think of deserting. They came from England, Holland, and Belgium, and they worked from early morning till late at night, with only a half day off every other week. But Edith Cavell had so filled their hearts with the ideals of nursing that they gloried in their profession.

They admired and respected Miss Cavell, even though they did not quite understand her. She was thin and frail, with an indomitable will. She carried her head high and walked with the carriage of a soldier, so that she seemed taller than she was. Sometimes she would play for them on the piano in the little sitting room, but though they gathered round and sang for her, they never felt intimate with her. At mealtimes she shared their meager food and sat silently—there was little conversation—and afterward she would stand at the door and nod to each one as they filed past. Then she

would return to her office or her rounds.

But the girls knew of a thousand instances of her kindness, too. She had helped one of the probationers who had got into trouble, she had saved another young girl from a disastrous situation, and when they tiptoed upstairs late at night in their stocking feet her voice would float out to them, "Put your shoes on, my dears, you will catch cold." And now they knew that she had undertaken this hazardous business of helping soldiers to leave the country.

What had brought her to this position of trust and danger? they wondered. Once in a while they would glimpse her, in her small office, the endless papers before her, her head resting on her thin, delicately boned hand, and they were sure she was thinking of her past. It was a strange story, and sometimes Edith Cavell pondered herself on the quirks of fate that had brought her, an Englishwoman, to make her life work in an alien country in wartime.

She remembered her childhood in the vicarage of Swardeston, a sleepy little town in rural England, where her father ministered to the people and her mother, a bright, warmhearted person, offset his dour nature by her laughter and her generous heart. Edith often walked with her dogs in the cemetery that adjoined the vicarage. She always had dogs, and even in war-ridden Belgium she kept her cherished Don and Jack close to her. She picked wild strawberries, and studied and played with her younger brother and sister and sang nursery rhymes to them. When she was sent away to Miss Margaret Gibson's School she studied hard, and it was through Miss Gibson that she became governess in a wealthy Belgian family.

They were quiet, happy years, but when she received word that her father was very ill she returned to England. For almost a year she took care of him. In that time a desire that had always been with her, but that she had not recognized, came to the surface. She would be a nurse!

At that time nursing was looked upon askance as a profession for a young woman. It had not been very many years since Florence Nightingale had encouraged nursing as a career. Patients and doctors were skeptical. The training was hard, the duties harder, the pay very low. On the Continent, no "proper" young lady went into nursing. If she did, her chances of getting married were canceled.

Edith Cavell was thirty-five when she decided to become a nurse. Anyone else would have said she was too old to begin training. But she became a student nurse at London Hospital. It was a noisy place in the midst of sooty buildings and near the docks. It smelled of carbolic acid, the cooking was poor, and the walls were grimy, whitewashed plaster.

As a "pink," or probationer, she slept with three other girls in a small cell-like room. Her days were filled with the most menial tasks. When the pinks weren't studying or tending the sick they scrubbed floors and polished brasswork. The matron found

Edith to be a good student who accepted her work cheerfully, and soon she was ministering to the feeble, the poor, the aged, the insane, and even the criminal of London.

With only two years' experience, Edith Cavell was given supervision over other nurses when a typhoid epidemic broke out. The hospitals were taxed to the limit, and afterward people said her work was outstanding. From there she became night superintendent at North St. Pancreas Infirmary, which took care of accident cases and especially of children. Later she was made Assistant Matron at Shoreditch Infirmary, a bleak place in a squalid district of London, and then at Fountain Hospital, Lower Tooting, and after that temporary Matron of the Ashton New Road District in Manchester.

There were many poor here, and nearby mills and mines furnished a constant supply of casualties. Many people remember Edith Cavell, in her flowing cape and with her black bag, hurrying through the streets on her errands of mercy. She lent clothes for newborn babies, found bedding and blankets and chairs and hot water bottles for those who needed them. They called her "the poor man's Nightingale," and her picture was in most homes. One of her nurses said, "Next to Miss Cavell, other women seem so weak—so thin."

It was about this time that the brilliant Dr. Depage set up his *Clinique* in Brussels. He had bought several houses side by side and turned them into a hospital which took care of all cases from maternity to mental. He needed nurses; he needed a supervisor. One of the prominent Belgians who sponsored the school was a *Mme.* Graux. Her son had married Marguerite Francois, for whom Edith Cavell had been governess years before. So it was through *Mme.* Graux that Edith Cavell was invited to come to Brussels and organize and direct a nursing school!

She knew it would not be an easy task. There were no nursing schools in Belgium—few, for that matter, in all of Europe. Nuns without medical training took care of most of the sick. Dr. Depage had another ideal; he wanted trained women for his own hospital and for the city.

Edith Cavell uniformed her first group of nine probationers in blue cotton dresses, white collars, high white aprons with white linen sleeves to cover the forearms, and little white caps—a far cry from the flowing black of the nun nurses. Soon the number of probationers grew to thirteen— girls from England, Holland, France, Switzerland, and even Germany.

The girls respected and trusted her. They thought she was strict, but just. They worked for her rare smile—but as the years went by and her work increased, and her wartime responsibilities mounted, the smile seldom came, though her composure never vanished. She was like a rock to them. She taught anatomy and preventive medicine and hygiene, illustrating her talks with drawings on the blackboard. She expected the best of them; with lives at stake, they must be careful and gentle, and know all they could. She had no patience with sloppy habits and faulty thinking.

The hospital prospered, even though there was never enough money, and the nursing school was crowded. Dr. Depage's wife helped him in his work and in the laboratory. Edith Cavell was proud of her girls and their work.

For herself she took on still more duties. It was almost as if she were trying to make up for years lost to nursing. She became Matron of the new St. Gilles Hospital, not far away from the *Clinique,* and also at St. Pierre and St. Jean, and at a special sanitarium that the energetic Dr. Depage had set up. Doctors thought so highly of her as a surgical nurse that she was in constant demand at major operations. She made daily rounds of the hospitals, she taught, she helped in surgery, and her responsibilities to hundreds of patients were added to her responsibility for her "girls" whom she was training.

By 1912 she could report that her school was furnishing nurses for three hospitals, three private clinics, twenty-four public schools, and thirteen kindergartens. The kindergartens were her special joy. She loved children and wished she had more time to give them. The walls of St. Gilles' nursery were painted blue and white, with pictures from Aesop's Fables along the walls.

Her students worried about her, she was so tired and frail. Finally they persuaded her to take a vacation and she went back to England to visit.

It was in August of that year, 1914, that war broke out. She might have stayed in England, but her duties, and her heart, called her back to Belgium. She never saw her mother again. Belgium was overrun by the conquering Germans, their gray uniforms were everywhere, the government left Brussels for Antwerp, the fortresses at Antwerp fell, people were fleeing to the country, the roads were clogged, the wounded began coming in. Edith Cavell was needed now more than ever, for Brussels had been declared defenseless.

She wrote, "I have seen suffering, poverty, and human wretchedness in the slums of London, but nothing I saw there hurts me the way it does to see these proud, gay, happy people humiliated and deprived of their men, their homes invaded by enemy soldiers quartered in them, their business ruined. I can only ask myself why, oh, why, should these innocent people be made to suffer like this?"

She was outspoken in conversations, too, and people worried about her, but Edith Cavell lifted her head high. "In times like these," she said, "when terror makes might seem right, there is a higher duty than prudence."

That was why she began hiding soldiers in her cellar; in the back rooms of the old houses that were the hospital. That is why she had her probationers put up packages of bread and milk, and herself led the hidden ones out of the city by devious routes, so that they might escape to Holland—and perhaps to England. That is why she

took on more and more men, whom patriots
brought to her, and kept them hidden till they
could be spirited away by *guides,* men who risked
their lives nightly to take others out of the country. The girls knew what was going on; they were
thrilled but unhappy, for they never knew, as the
months wore on, when they would be caught. And
they feared for their directress. But the directress
herself was fearless.

Food grew scarcer and scarcer. The empty lot
across from the *Clinique* was turned into a potato
field where people labored every day. But who
were these people? Among them might be a spy,
keeping his eye on the comings and goings at the
Clinique. Who were some of the men who applied
for refuge? They spoke French or English . . . but
were they French or English?

Sister Wilkins, Edith Cavell's valuable assistant, was sure one of their refugees was an in-
former. His name, as he gave it, was Quin, and
several times he had followed one of the nurses as

she crossed the city to leave a message at the home of a patriot.

In July Miss Cavell accepted nine English soldiers who had been found in the woods near a chateau by a schoolteacher patriot, Louise Thuliez. They had been there only a short time before two German officers arrived to talk to Edith Cavell. They went into her office, and Sister Wilkins spirited the Englishmen, half dressed, into the basement and then into the garden and over a stone wall to a vacant house in the rear. Other nurses were gathering up magazines in English and French and hiding them under bathtubs. Secret papers went into a storage tank, but one of the officers cried, *"Verboten!"* The nurses recognized him as one of the men who some time ago had come to discuss renting a room.

The directress's office was turned upside down. Pictures and family portraits were torn from the walls, cups and saucers smashed in the cupboards, floor boards pried loose. They did not find what

they were after—but a German guard came to live at the *Clinique;* he sat, puffing a cigar, in a little room near the front door where he could see everyone who came and went.

It was the beginning of the end. The *Clinique* and all who lived and worked there were under suspicion. The girls, not one of whom thought of leaving their directress in her trouble, felt, they said, as if they must fall on their knees to her; so sweet and calm and strong she was, so unyielding in her sense of what was right to do.

All over Brussels people were being arrested . . . housewives, shopkeepers, architects . . . whoever had assisted in any way to offset the cruelty of the Germans or helped men escape to neutral country. Miss Cavell and her devoted staff were getting ready to move into a new hospital which, in spite of the war, had been built and made ready for them. It was three-thirty on the fifth of August. Three men, not in uniform, entered the old clinic. "We want to look at some furniture," they said. It seemed a reasonable request, for they had old things to dispose of.

Without warning, one of the men leveled a revolver at the head of Sister Wilkins, pushed her into a side room, and another man went off to find the directress. He found her in an upstairs pantry arranging flowers.

When he brought her down, the nurses were in terror. But Edith Cavell said calmly, "Don't be sad, my children. Everything will be all right. I'll be back soon."

They took Sister Wilkins and Edith Cavell to the commandant. Sister Wilkins denied everything; she did not know what was going on, she did not know the men who had supplied the report, she turned their questions aside until they were tired of questioning her and let her return to the *Clinique*.

But they put Edith Cavell in solitary confinement in St. Gilles prison. No one was allowed to see her, although food could be sent in. The girls

saved their pennies and sent her roses and chrys-
anthemums, and much later she wrote them a
loving letter, bidding them be of good cheer. She
asked about Sister Wilkins and her beloved dog
Jack; she asked them to study hard so that they
could pass their examinations with credit to themselves and to her. She felt, she said, that she would
be back soon.

But she never came back. They put her on trial,
with the others, and she calmly acknowledged that
she had helped men escape. She made a written
confession in which she told exactly how many
and who they were and how much money she had
supplied them with. She would deny nothing. Her
defending lawyer was in despair, for she made it
impossible for him to build up a case to save her.

She read her Bible and wrote in her prayer book
and wrote to her nurses and saw the visiting clergyman with a quiet, composed face. Her bearing
was as erect as ever, her eyes as calm, her faith
unshaken.

On a chill morning in October, at five o'clock, they drove Edith Cavell to the prison yard. She was neatly dressed in her cape and black hat. They tied her arms and set her against the white wall, and fired bullets into her body.

It was quickly over. Edith Cavell died as she had lived, quietly and bravely.

But in one sense, it was not over and never will be. Word flashed around the world that a brave and wonderful woman had been killed. People wept, men fought to join the colors to avenge her death. Hospitals were built in her name. Her body was brought home to England on a battleship, and a statue stands, in Trafalgar Square, as a constant reminder of her valor. Here the tall, gaunt figure, with the beautiful face and searching eyes and flowing nurse's uniform, reminds everyone who sees it of the quality of the human spirit.

"Patriotism is not enough," Edith Cavell said, from her heart. "I must have no hatred or bitterness for anyone."

In Time of War

DOROTHY DAVIS

The world she knew, and had always known, was Shanghai. From the day of her birth, she had been surrounded by the sights and sounds and smells of the Orient. Yet Dorothy Davis' parents had made a home which was a little bit of America for their two daughters. There were Chinese servants, and there were lovely examples of Chinese art and craftsmanship in every room, but

72

the life was the life of an American family.

Dorothy's father had been born in China, too, and spoke the Shanghai dialect fluently, but by the time his daughters were born many of the Chinese had mastered some of the English language. All too swiftly the girls' *amahs* would learn English while Dorothy and her sister Eva Grace, who were supposed to learn Chinese from them, found little opportunity. One time a new *amah* was engaged—one who knew no English at all. Now, surely, Mrs. Davis thought, the girls would begin to learn Chinese. But the Chinese nurse, eager to learn, was always asking for words in English.

The girls went to an American school in Shanghai, and one of their studies was French. They decided it would be great fun to tell the *amah* French words instead of English ones, so that all the time she thought she was learning English, she was really learning French!

Their home was next to the country club, and

Dorothy learned to ride early. She would get up at five in the morning to go out on her horse, and one time she confided to her mother that she thought horseback riding was more fun than boys or parties. There were Sunday morning waffle breakfasts in her spacious home afterward, and then a swim in the country club pool. She and Eva Grace were both good swimmers.

Dorothy's mother had a sister who had been a trained nurse in World War I, serving in Europe before the United States went into the war, and when Dorothy was still in her early teens, their Aunt Dora came to China to visit them.

People commented on the physical resemblance between Dorothy and her aunt, and her mother thought there was even more of a resemblance than that, for Dorothy was already putting all her desires for the future into the idea of nursing. Her parents were not anxious to have her take up the career. For one thing, they did not feel that she was strong enough, and when she had graduated from the Shanghai American School, the family doctor concurred.

"You are too anemic," he told Dorothy. "Wait awhile, and build yourself up. Nursing is a strenuous career, and if you go into it, you will need all the strength you have."

So she stayed at home, taking lessons in art and literature and, the following year, in stenography and typing. She even got a job, keeping her fingers crossed where her spelling was concerned.

But by the spring of 1937 she was on her way! Back in the States she entered a camp for the summer, where she had one of the most pleasant experiences of her life. The riding instructor having broken his leg at the beginning of the camp season, Dorothy was given the opportunity to take his place, so she had her fill of riding that summer. That was not all, for the New York City stable, which had the riding concession at the camp, asked her to keep on with her riding. All through the three years of her nurse's training, she was

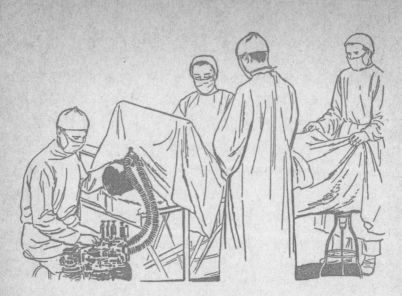

able to enjoy her favorite sport.

Dorothy loved her years at the Presbyterian Hospital School of Nursing, and that love was reflected in her marks, for she was always in the top tenth of her class. During those years she realized that she would always prefer actual nursing to executive or organizational work, and that, of all the nursing experience, she liked being a surgical nurse best of all.

But there was disturbing news from home during those three years. In the month of August, following her departure for the States, the Japanese moved into Peking and from that time on the world of business in China was in a state of chaos. In the end, her parents lost everything they had.

Eva Grace, in the meanwhile, had finished her business course at the Katharine Gibbs School, and for a while Mrs. Davis came to the States while Mr. Davis went to Manila, in the Philippines, to investigate his prospects for opening a business there and making a new start.

In the spring of 1941 Dorothy went to Manila. By this time her family was settled there, and she joined them in their apartment. After taking her examination for nurse's registration in the Philippines, she was engaged as a civilian employee of the Army Nurse Corps at Sternberg General Hospital, a military hospital. It did not take her long to decide that she wanted to join the Army Nurse Corps, and she made her application as soon as possible. Her final papers were sent to the United States in November of that year.

There was an influx of Army nurses at about that time, and she was laid off, but when the sneak attack on Pearl Harbor was made, she was called back at once.

Those were tense days for the people of Manila. The Japanese advance was unbelievably swift. Now Dorothy was going on duty at Sternberg Hospital at seven in the evening, and she seldom got home before noon of the following day. Yet, even then, she could not sleep, for the shelling was heavy, and the Davises' apartment house was quite close to the water. The ships in the harbor were under constant bombing attack, and the house shook with every explosion. All the tenants had to crowd into the basement for shelter. Dorothy was lucky if she got two hours of sleep before it was time to go on duty again at the hospital.

Just before Christmas the U. S. Army made Manila an open city, in hopes it would be saved, and they evacuated all the seriously wounded cases that they could. Dorothy begged to be allowed to go to Bataan with the Army nurses but when Christmas Eve arrived, she found, instead, that she had been left in sole charge of the hospital and several hundred wounded men. There were a few Filipino girls, who spoke little English, to help her, but no doctor and no other nurses.

That was a night of horror. In the complete darkness of the blackout, with no way of calling for help when she needed it (the telephones were not working, and transportation was at a standstill), with sick and wounded crying for assistance, she tried to be everywhere at once. One of the patients rose from his bed in an effort to help her and dropped dead at her feet.

Her family waited through that terrible Christmas morning, wondering what had happened to her, for she had said, as she left the evening before, "If I'm not back tomorrow morning, that means I'll have received permission to go to Bataan with the others."

Morning came, but Dorothy did not appear, and they could only suppose that she had managed to get permission, after all. The hours passed slowly, while their thoughts centered about Dorothy, wondering when they would see her again. At noon the doorbell rang, and there was a young officer with Dorothy clinging, exhausted, to his arm. There was something to be thankful for, after all, on this sad Christmas morning, for they were together again.

The Japanese came into the city early on New Year's Day after a forced march from the south of the island, and the Davises, like other Americans and allied nationalities, were given only a brief time in which to arrange their affairs. They were told to report for registration, bringing food supplies for three days, and they were allowed only one suitcase for clothing and other possessions.

Then began the long ordeal of the internment camp. They were lodged at Santo Tomas, one of the oldest universities in the Orient. At first there were no beds, and people slept on their blankets on the floor. The sanitary conditions were completely inadequate for such numbers of people, and almost at once there was illness.

There were injuries, too, for no one had had time to prepare for this sort of life. They were soon coming to Dorothy with cuts and bruises. Despite her own fatigue, Dorothy attended to them gladly.

Since she was the only person known to be a nurse, she was put in charge of the nursing service from the beginning. Eva Grace worked with her, and the two girls began canvassing the 3,500 internees to discover who had had any nursing experience. It was not difficult to foresee the need for help.

She put the notebook containing these names with her blanket and pillow, for there was no place to store anything, of course. It was bad enough when the blanket and pillow were stolen, for that meant she had to sleep on the damp stone floor without protection of any kind. But the theft of the notebook meant that all the work of gathering names had to be done over again.

Within the crowded space of the university, it was hard to find a place for a clinic and dispensary. There were five moves before it was decided to take over a clapboard building which had been used for the teaching of electrical engineering. It was filled with heavy machinery and equipment but a team of men internees managed to remove some of this. In between what remained, Dorothy says, " . . . we draped (!) about fifty beds."

She had help now, for a few days after their arrival at the camp several experienced nurses had come in. They had been supervisors of mission hospitals in India, China, and Hong Kong. Dorothy was happy to see them, and she would have been glad to have one of them take over, but they refused. "You started this," they told her,

"and it is all yours. We are only here to help and advise."

There were many more problems than the lack of space. At first there was the problem of beds and medical supplies. They were able to get permission to receive beds from the Red Cross Emergency Unit in Manila, but when trucks arrived with the beds, the guards would not let them enter. Over and over the trucks returned until they finally got past the front gate.

Now they had some low cast-iron beds, but there was so much else that was lacking. There were very few bedpans, and only one or two basins with which to bathe the patients, who numbered about seventy-five by then. And there was little water with which to bathe them even if they had had the basins, for all the water had to be carried from the kitchen. It was cold water, and there was no way of heating it for a long time.

Drugs were needed. For the first few days they were allowed to send some men out to Manila

drug stores to get supplies. These men wore red
arm bands to identify them as internees, and they
had to be careful not to speak to anyone except
on the business for which they were sent.

The confusion and crowding were constant. It
was hard to get any sleep at all, for there was no
privacy and no quiet. Dorothy asked if she might
have assistance from the Philippine Red Cross,
and this was granted. Two Filipino nurses were
allowed to come into the camp each evening and
take over the night duty. Later, when the number
of patients increased, as they did steadily throughout the months, several more nurses were permitted to come in during the daytime as well. And
all the time there was a certain amount of training of girls, so that there would be a number of
them available for aide work.

It was certainly a different kind of hospital
from those Dorothy had been accustomed to.
Almost everything had to be improvised from the
materials at hand, and even these were in short

supply. One of the most interesting of the impro-
visations was the way in which they made diet
tickets for their patients. A sheet was torn into
small pieces. Some of these were dipped into gen-
tian violet, some into picric acid, some into
Mercurochrome, while others were left white.
These were tied onto the beds. The purple rags
meant "soft diet," the yellow ones "special diet,"
the red ones "liquid diet," and the white ones
"regular diet." Best of all, they could be used over
and over again.

There was one Bunsen burner, left from the
college equipment, on which to heat the patients'
food or the necessary hot water. A large religious
mural found a practical use as well as a spiritual
one by serving as a partition. The four doctors
who were assigned to the clinic had numbered
chairs, and some of the boys cut down a tree and
made wooden numbers which were handed to the
waiting patients, so that they would see the doctor
in the proper order. As the hospital grew, a special

dental clinic was set up, and also one for physiotherapy.

That first month of organization was a terribly
strenuous one, and not long afterward Dorothy
came down with rheumatic fever. Sleeping on the
damp floor without a blanket was undoubtedly a
contributing factor. Fatigue was another. She was
very ill and for a while they despaired of her life.
But her spirit was strong, and she was eager to
get back to her chosen work as soon as possible.

Unfortunately, she went back too soon and had
a relapse. In the twenty-one months that she spent
in the internment camp, Dorothy not only suffered
from the effects of the rheumatic fever, but also
had an emergency appendectomy, and such a bad
throat that she had to have her tonsils removed.

Many operations were done at St. Luke's Hospital in Manila, and patients had to have permission to be sent out for them. Both of Dorothy's
operations, however, were done at the Philippine General Hospital by Filipino surgeons. An

indication of how the Filipinos felt about the
Japanese internment of Americans is shown by
the fact that these men would take no pay for their
work. The Filipinos were wonderful to Dorothy,
as they were to other Americans. Still, it was hard
to be alone and ill, harder still when there was the
ever-present worry about her family and their
welfare.

She never really gave herself time to recu-
perate, always starting to work long before she
should have. For a while she was in the children's
hospital, but again she overdid, and that time she
was supposed to stay flat on her back for a long,
long time.

Dorothy, however, was a nurse through and
through. Though she lay obediently upon her
narrow cot, she was incapable of centering her
thoughts upon herself. On one side of her was a
girl who was also laid low with rheumatic fever.
Dorothy thought up ways of keeping her enter-
tained so that she would remain quiet and rest

as she was supposed to.

Then food poisoning struck the t.b. ward. From the very beginning the internees had been afflicted by various kinds of digestive ailments. The poor quality of the food, the dirt, the clouds of flies, all brought on many attacks of gastro-enteritis. Dysentery and amebic dysentery were common, and insects and parasites brought further troubles to the population of the Santo Tomas camp.

But this was something sudden and drastic. Every nurse on duty was called to help, so that there were none left in the other parts of the hospital. Dorothy took over the care of the ward in which she lay, as a matter of course.

One of the women whose cot was near hers was desperately ill. She was waiting for permission to be sent out to a hospital for an intestinal operation. In the meanwhile a system of improvised tubes was keeping her alive. Something went wrong in the middle of the night; the tubes became tangled and a real emergency arose. There was no one to handle it—no one who was well, that is—so Dorothy rose from her cot and took over, watching all night to make sure that the woman would live. And, despite the seriousness of her illness and her near escape from death that night, the woman did live. Dorothy knew, when she went back to her cot again, that she had saved another life.

It had been a great help when, in March of that first year, the Navy nurses who were quartered in Santa Scolastica were sent into the internment camp of Santo Tomas. Then, in July and August, their numbers were augmented by sixty-eight Army nurses who came from Corregidor, and Bataan, and Davao. Maude Davison, who had been the Army Chief Nurse on Bataan, took over the running of the hospital nursing service, and from then on it was run as much like an Army hospital as possible.

All the civilian nurses, with the exception of Dorothy and one other, then withdrew from active nursing in the camp, and Dorothy moved in with the Army nurses. How she wished that her papers could have come before the fall of Manila! Now she did not know whether she had been accepted by the Army Nurse Corps or not, but she *felt* like an Army nurse, and bunking with them made the feeling stronger.

The nurses lived in four rooms, each one allowed a space of forty inches by six feet. This was small quarters for the accommodation of a cot and whatever small possessions a woman might have, but it also had to include space for an aisle, otherwise they would not have been able to move about at all!

But, although she slept in the nurses' quarters, Dorothy still saw as much of her family as possible. Everyone had duties to perform, and the simplest details of survival in the camp took a great deal of time and ingenuity. Her sister, Eva Grace, had become secretary to the American chief of the Executive Committee and her work was difficult, and sometimes dangerous. The two girls saw each other whenever they could, but the starvation diet was beginning to tell. It was hard enough to find sufficient energy for the day's work; after a while, there was none left over. Yet some inner strength upheld them.

When word swept through the camp that 120 American and Canadian internees were to be repatriated on the *Gripsholm,* there was terrific excitement. The details were slow in coming out, but at last they learned that those to be sent home to the United States would be the very ill, and that they were to be accompanied, wherever possible, by a member of their families.

Dorothy had never thought of herself as one of those who would be freed, although the camp doctors had, from the beginning of her illness, asked the Japanese to repatriate her at the earliest possible time. When her name was posted, with that of her mother, she could scarcely believe it.

On September 26, 1943, she and her mother

parted from the rest of the family and began the long trip home. She had no belongings to bother about, with one exception. Throughout all these months Dorothy had kept her diploma from the Presbyterian Hospital School of Nursing with her wherever she went. Now she took it with her again —her most prized possession.

They left in the gray dawn and were taken in trucks to a train. The slow, fatiguing trip took all day to Lingayen Gulf in northern Luzon. There they were taken by lighter to a small Japanese ship, meant to accommodate three hundred people, but which was already crowded with fifteen hundred allied nationals being evacuated from Japan and China.

They stopped at Hong Kong, Saigon, and Singapore for more repatriates, and eventually reached Goa, on the west coast of India in mid-October, where they transferred to the *Gripsholm*. It was the first time they had seen the United States flag in twenty-two months!

Dorothy had done something important before she left Santo Tomas. Knowing that the liberated internees would be allowed to take nothing in writing except a few addresses, she had set herself to memorize the names of the seventy-five or more Army and Navy nurses who were interned at the camp. When she arrived in New York early in December, she was able to give these names to the authorities. For the first time, the Army and Navy were able to learn what had happened to the brave nurses who had been captured by the

Japanese early in the war.

Perhaps Dorothy's greatest thrill on returning home came when she learned that her acceptance as an Army nurse had been mailed to her before Manila fell. Through the fortunes of war, it had never reached her. Now she entered the Army Nurse Corps at once, and her first request was for overseas service in the Pacific.

Instead, she was sent to Walter Reed Hospital in Washington, D. C., where she served as surgical nurse for many brain operations. Whenever she asked to be sent overseas, the reply was that nurses were always kept here in the States for two years after a return from duty.

"But," Dorothy retorted, "you tell me I was *not* an Army nurse in the Philippines because I hadn't received my papers. So, if I was not an Army nurse then, I need not wait for two years before being sent overseas."

Eventually she won the argument. Her mother, who had become Assistant Director of Residences at Adelphi College for the cadet nurses, did not want her to go.

"You're not strong enough yet," she told Dorothy, knowing, even as she said the words, that they would have little effect. It was bad enough to wonder if Mr. Davis and Eva Grace still lived, without having to see her remaining daughter shipped back into the theater of war.

She would have been doubly worried if she could have known what was to happen on the way. Dorothy's ship was torpedoed at Hollandia. Fortunately the torpedo was a dud, and everyone was transferred to another ship, which took them to Leyte. The great push was on, and our men were heading north at phenomenal speed.

Now Dorothy's hopes began to rise. As distances went in the Pacific, Leyte was not too far from Manila. They had scarcely disembarked at Leyte, and were getting settled in their tents for the night, when Dorothy heard that a number of nurses were to be detached from the group the next day and would be flown directly into Manila with some high-ranking officers. She could barely contain herself until she heard the names of the girls chosen to go.

She was not among them! All that night she cried softly into her pillow, for this was something she had had her heart set on. How much longer would she have to wait now?

At five in the morning her commanding officer touched her lightly on the shoulder. "Can you get ready quickly?" she was asked. "You are to be one of the nurses flown into Manila this morning."

Dorothy came erect like a released spring. "But I thought—" she cried, "my name wasn't one of those—"

"I know," her colonel said. "But we didn't tell you last night because we were afraid you would be too excited to sleep!"

And so, on the eighth of February, 1945, more than three years after she had entered Santo Tomas for the first time, Dorothy came into it again, this time in a truck filled with other Army nurses. She was recognized at once, and word went out over the loud-speakers to her father and sister that she had arrived.

That was a reunion to bring tears to everyone who saw it. Dorothy was horrified to see how woefully thin they had become. But the spirit which had never weakened still shone brightly from their eyes, as it had shone steadfastly from hers.

Not many stories of the war had as happy an ending as Dorothy's. Married to an officer of the Signal Corps, and the mother of three lovely children, she has continued to give of herself through her nursing in an Army hospital. Not many people have known such privation and such riches in life, but through all her experiences, tragic or happy, Dorothy has kept her heart open to the needs of others.

The Greatest Gift

FRANCESCA CABRINI

Francesca Cabrini was a quiet little girl, strictly brought up by Rosa, a much older sister, for she was the youngest of thirteen. She lived on a farm in Lombardy, Italy, where she had been born in 1850, and she did not seem too different from other children, except for one thing: She wanted to be a missionary and go to China!

Rosa had graduated from a normal school and

ran a small private school where little Francesca
had her first lessons. Later she went to school at a
convent for five years. She learned to sew and
embroider, and she had a good grounding in
academic studies as well, so that, on graduation,
she had a certificate to teach. But she did not want
to teach at that time; she wanted to enter the
convent. It was a great disappointment to her
when she was refused due to her health.

After that she stayed at home for a while. When
her parents had died, there were left only her
sister, Rosa, and a brother, Giovanni. Her brother
ran the farm, although he would have preferred
to teach, and later he did become a renowned edu-
cator in Argentina. Rosa, strangely softened by
her parents' death, was much kinder and sweeter
to little Francesca. The three of them lived
together very simply.

When a smallpox epidemic struck the area,
Rosa went about caring for the stricken with un-
daunted fervor. Francesca, on the other hand, had

always had an aversion to nursing the sick. Yet, when the emergency arose, she went into the work wholeheartedly, refusing to let the sights and smells of the disease disturb her. Before the epidemic was over, Francesca came down with smallpox herself. Then Rosa's love for her sister came to the fore. She nursed her steadily and selflessly, so that there was not a single scar to show later.

When Francesca was well, she agreed to teach for a while in a village two miles away, so that the regular teacher, who was sick, would not lose her job. The "for a while" became two years.

Although her desire for missionary work in China had never wavered, it seemed that life was determined to divert her energies into other streams of service. Asked by her pastor to go to Codogno to try to bring some order to a chaotically run orphanage, she went for two weeks and stayed two years. Then, because it was asked of her, she took the habit and stayed on another six years. But things were different after that. She had the training of a handful of novitiates who were to be with her when her dreams came true and she founded her own Institute of the Sacred Heart.

All her life she was to found schools and academies and orphanages, and these were the closest to her heart for many years. That early distaste for nursing had not been completely conquered, and the thought of founding hospitals was probably furthest from her mind.

One time, when she was visiting in Rome, the troubles of the "dispersed" Italians in the United States was brought to her attention. Our country was receiving thousands of Italian immigrants every year—poor people who had spent their all in the effort to reach a country where they were sure they would soon become rich. There was so little opportunity in the Italy of those days. Yet, when these poor people came to America, their lot was not bettered. Many of them became slaves of the peonage system, whereby the men who had

advanced them money for their passage kept them
in constant debt by underpaying them and charg-
ing huge rates of interest.

They were crowded into slums, where dirt and
disease soon took a terrible toll. They were un-
educated; most of them had had no chance to
learn English and could not even make their plight
known. When they were sick, they were sent to
the worst of our hospitals and in many cases
treated more like criminals than sick people.
Because there was no way of communicating with
the doctors and nurses, they were given only the
necessary treatment. A smile or a kind word in
the language they knew was too much to expect.

As a result, most of the Italian immigrants were
afraid to go to a hospital under any circumstances,
and this attitude grew stronger as more and more
of them came to New York City and fell victim
to poverty, disease, fear, and helplessness.

In 1889, when Francesca was asked to go to
New York, her doctor was sure she had only two

years to live. But this indomitable woman was one who thrived on difficulties and was always willing to attack the impossible. When she came to this country, she was not only in poor health, but she was without material resources and did not even know how to speak the English language. There was no place waiting to receive her and the few nuns she had brought with her from her institute.

Yet, within a few weeks, by dint of hard work, begging, and her intuitive sense of what was needed, she had already started a small day school in the Italian quarter of the city, and she was soon to found an orphanage as well.

The last thing she had thought of doing, however, was to found a hospital. All of her work, and she was now past forty, had been connected with education and orphanages. But in 1891, she was asked to take charge of a hospital in New York which was running into difficulties.

Francesca was tempted to refuse and might have done so. She had no experience in running

hospitals, and besides, she had always shrunk from nursing the sick. But she went one day to visit some Italian patients in one of the public hospitals of New York. This was a custom of hers, to try to bring comfort to those who were ill and alone in a strange land.

A young man, who had been ill for a very long time, brought out a crumpled letter he had received from Italy three months before. "Will you read it for me, Mother?" he asked, in an anxious voice. "I do not know how to read, and no one here knows Italian."

She opened the letter with trepidation. The poor and illiterate did not usually receive letters unless they contained serious news. For a moment she hesitated, when she had read the contents, for she did not want to hurt the young man who was already suffering. Yet she knew he would feel worse if he did not know. And so, slowly and simply, she told him his mother had died.

This incident must have come back to her again

and again, and perhaps it was only one of many which made her agree to take over the small Italian hospital on East 129th Street. Certainly no one knew better than she that the Italians in New York needed a hospital. And she knew, too, that if left to themselves, they would do little to supply the need.

At this time, Italians had no sense of national unity. There were innumerable factions, each one at odds with the others. Funds had been collected previously for the founding of a Garibaldi Hospital, but through the years most of the money had slipped through various hands, and there was not much left.

The hospital on East 129th Street was a small place which had been managed by the Fathers of St. Charles Borromeo. It had run into money difficulties which were so great that by the time Francesca agreed to take over, there was no chance to pay off the debts. At this point the city government ordered the hospital closed.

Francesca planned to put the twenty-five patients in Bellevue Hospital, and she did transfer fifteen of them there, but then a strange thing happened. The remaining ten patients struck! They insisted that they wanted to stay with her.

Now she really had to do something and, with her customary competence and faith, she set about it at once. She found two houses on Twelfth Street, and with the meager sum of $250.00 given her by five men, she was able to pay a month's rent and to buy ten iron beds. There was no money left over for mattresses, and so the nuns sat on the floor and made them. Francesca cut out the sheets from a bolt of cloth. Food was sent in from a restaurant around the corner for the first week, and the hospital was in business!

There was no water at first, and that had to be brought in. There was no gas for cooking, but there was a coal stove in the one large room which served as a ward, and on this the sisters made soup. Their medical supplies consisted of a dozen bottles of medicine, but it was not long before the first gifts began to flow in.

Francesca's nuns were not nurses. They had had no professional training, and, indeed, their order was not prepared for this sort of thing at all. But word went around that they were kind and thoughtful. They lacked all sorts of appliances and supplies, but the first requisite of good nursing was theirs: a selfless devotion to their patients.

One of Francesca's inspirations came in the naming of the new institution. "Let's call it the Columbus Hospital," she said.

The nuns were surprised. They thought that a religious name might be better, and they wondered at her choice.

"This is the year 1892," she reminded them. "It is just exactly four hundred years since Columbus discovered America. Italians are proud of him, and he was, after all, the very first Italian immigrant, wasn't he?"

They laughed and agreed. But Francesca had

another reason, as well. "If we call it by a religious name," she said, "we will have the anti-clerical faction of the Italians against us. Just as, when they tried to raise money for the Garibaldi Hospital, the clerical faction would not support it. But if we call this the Columbus Hospital, *all* the Italians will think of it as theirs."

She was right. Before long, her nuns were even being called the Sisters of Columbus. Despite their own poverty, the first patients they took in were those who could pay nothing for their services. But perhaps it was this very fact which brought them help so soon. Their head physician was Dr. Keane, who not only contributed his services but would not permit any doctor on the hospital staff to charge.

Soon donations began to arrive. Money and equipment, both sorely needed, were eagerly accepted. Better still, some of the doctors sent those of their patients who could pay, so that they began to be self-supporting. Best of all, the re-

mainder of the sum which had been collected for
the Garibaldi Hospital was turned over to them.
Now they were on their feet. Now they could see
their way clear.

By September, Francesca felt she could leave
for Italy where she stayed for two years. When she
came back, she found Columbus Hospital not
only thriving but officially recognized by the
Italians in New York. Perhaps one of the reasons
why it had already found a place in their hearts
was because the sisters had accepted the care of
two sailors from an Italian warship. The sailors
had had typhoid, and no one else had been willing
to take them in. Neither could they be left on
the warship where there was danger of contagion.

Admiral Manghi came to thank the sisters in
person for their kindness to his men. This was
splendid publicity, and the former tenement was
soon crowded to its doors with patients. The
Italian Consul General, following this episode,
arranged that any sick Italian sailor, serving on a

merchant ship, would be received by the sisters for a flat sum.

Almost the first thing Francesca had to do when she returned to this country was to look for larger quarters. As she had done in the past when looking for suitable buildings for her orphanages or schools, she walked up and down the streets, looking at any and every building which might possibly do. And, as had happened before, she found just what she needed.

The old Post Graduate Hospital on East 20th Street was being offered by the city for sixty thousand dollars. This was a real bargain price, and one which Francesca recognized as such at once. She set about raising the money to buy it. With a loan from the Emigrant Savings Bank, and one from the secretary of her medical board, she succeeded.

There would be room for many more patients now—the hospital had space for one hundred beds—but there were a number of alterations and renovations necessary before it could be opened for patients. The sister made these themselves. But in the meanwhile, they still slept in the attic of the old building, where the rain often came in through a hole in the roof.

As a sign of their approval the Italians in New York City began raising funds for Francesca's Columbus Hospital. She had been right—the name was one which appealed to all factions. Groceries and canned goods in quantity began to come in. And then the final seal of approval was given by the State of New York when, in March, 1895, it consented to its legal incorporation.

Eight years later, Francesca went to Chicago to found a Columbus Hospital there. She took with her two young nuns, and she stayed, for a while, at the home of a Dr. Lagorio, who was in charge of the Pasteur Institute. It was he, in company with the archbishop and the Servite Fathers, who had urged her to come.

She came, as always, with nothing. Before she

could even think of beginning, there were funds to be raised, and she and her two nuns went out early every morning to beg for money.

It was snowing on that April day when she first saw the North Shore Hotel. A gray stone building, it faced Lincoln Park, and the lake lay beyond. The setting was beautiful, and the six-story building had been one of Chicago's most fashionable hotels. The archbishop felt that she had found the very thing for her hospital. He was not even too dismayed by the price—$160,000.

"How much have you collected?" he asked.

"One thousand dollars," she told him.

"Mother, Mother! One thousand dollars will not get you very far!" he cried and burst out laughing.

Perhaps it was fantastic, but Francesca knew that the money would come in if it had to. She admitted that if left to herself, she would probably not have undertaken the task. "I have always made my steps accord with the length of my legs," she said. But, since the archbishop wanted her to do it—expected her to do it, in fact—she was willing to try.

She managed to gather in ten thousand dollars. Some of it came to her in dimes, some in larger gifts. When she had this sum, however, she was free to go ahead. But first she made sure that everything was being done in good order. The owners of the property, with an expansive gesture, had said that the property extended the whole length of the block. Before she signed any papers, Francesca wanted to be sure just what that meant, so she and her two young nuns went out one morning early with string, chalk, and a notebook.

The policeman on the beat was astounded to see the nuns bending down, holding the pieces of string out straight, making chalk marks on the sidewalk, and then jotting down something in the notebook. But, strange as these actions were, they were to pay off in the end. When Francesca was given the papers to sign later that morning, she glanced down at the figures.

"You told me," she said calmly, "that I would have the whole length of the block. But you are not giving me that, according to these figures. You have cut off a strip twenty-five feet wide."

A strip as large as that would have been big enough for two houses. The owners tried bluster. Francesca simply looked at them. "I have had it measured," she said at last. "If you like, we will have it measured again."

They were defeated, and they knew it.

She had trouble, too, with the workmen and the contractors who had been engaged to make the alterations which would transform it from a hotel into a hospital. Unfortunately, she had to leave several sisters in charge while she went out of town, and when she returned, she found the handsome building little more than a shell.

Without a moment's delay, Francesca told the contractors that they were dismissed, and from then on she supervised the work herself. Her

lawyer, John Willard Newman, was able to see
to it that the bills for unnecessary work were
repudiated, and with her energetic self on constant
duty, the work went on swiftly. On April 26, 1905,
Chicago's Columbus Hospital was opened.

Four years later, Francesca realized that Chicago needed another hospital. Columbus Hospital
was extremely successful from the economic
standpoint, but she felt that another place was
needed where the poor of Italian birth could be
cared for by Italian-speaking nurses and doctors.
Its expenses would be met by the profits of the
first hospital, as she planned it.

According to her custom, she went on foot to
look for a suitable building, and she found it, too,
in a snowstorm, in an exclusive residential area
near Vermont Park. This was a large private
home, but Francesca already saw it as a
shelter for the sick poor, and alterations were
begun at once. She moved with her usual swift-
ness and decision, and the people in the neighbor-

hood suddenly realized that there was to be a hospital in their midst. They did not like the idea.

There were two attempts at sabotage which would have discouraged anyone else, but Francesca had a solution. When her nuns, worried by the attempts to oust them with water and with fire, suggested that dynamite might be included in the next attempt, Francesca only smiled. "We won't wait until the renovations are finished," she said. "We'll move in now." For she was quite sure that once the place had patients in it, no further attempts would be made to destroy it.

Sixteen patients were brought over from the hospital immediately. Within a few days, there was not room for one more. The Italians of Chicago responded to her appeals, and gifts of money and equipment began to arrive. Another hospital was on its way to success.

That same year, Mother Cabrini became an American citizen. She had meant to become one for a long time, but she had always been so very busy. Always on the move, always engaged in some large project—if not two or three—her energy and accomplishments were contradicted by her frail health and feminine manner. Theodore Maynard, in *Too Small a World* describes her as a "quiet whirlwind."

In 1912, she felt that her Columbus Hospital in New York was much too small, and she made plans for a larger one to be built. She began collecting for it in Italy while she was there and even managed to obtain the promise of an annual subsidy from the Italian government. It was not very easy to raise the money in New York itself. But Francesca was never one to wait until the money for an undertaking was in hand. She felt sure that it would come in, and she blithely went ahead with her plans. She engaged a young architect to design for her a ten-story building, the one which now houses Columbus Hospital on East 19th Street.

Three years later she was turning the former Perry Hotel in Seattle into a hospital for physiotherapy and electrotherapy treatments. Later this, too, became a general hospital, but she had barely established it in 1917 when her health, which had been failing steadily, broke. Her nuns put her to bed when she got back to Chicago.

But even during her illness, she was working and planning. On one of her drives into the country, she decided that it would be a good idea to buy a farm so that her Chicago hospitals could have milk, eggs, and chickens at less than they had had to pay, and she soon bought a farm at Park Ridge. No doubt she had many smiling memories of her childhood when she saw to the purchase of the cows herself.

Francesca died near the end of that year, after a lifetime of astounding accomplishment. She had always gone beyond her strength, but her unflagging spirit had upheld her in her work. Francesca Cabrini—Mother Cabrini, as she was called by countless people she had helped—became the first United States citizen to be canonized.

Lady Légionnaire

GENEVIÈVE
DE GALARD-TERRAUBE

There was mud everywhere. The constant movement of men and machines, as well as the heavy bombardment, had pulverized the earth, and rain had turned the soil into a slippery, slimy mass of muck. Geneviève de Galard-Terraube thought that here in Indochina the mud must be the worst there was, for the rains came often.

She gazed about her at the flooded lowlands of

122

Dien Bien Phu where the French troops had dug in against the attacking Vietminhs. Some of the bunkers where the men lived were knee-deep in water. Despite the heat, she shivered a little. She had not dreamed, when she set out last night, that she would be stranded here upon this beleaguered plot of land. But although the hospital plane on which she was flight nurse had landed in the darkness and had loaded nineteen badly wounded men on board, unseen damage from barbed wire prevented the take-off. The wounded were carried back to the underground hospital on the run, and she herself had had to dash for shelter.

The hospital had literally been dug out of the earth. There were mud steps leading down to it, and the floor was ankle deep in mud. There were only three rooms: an operating room, an emergency-treatment room, and an X-ray room. That is, there *had* been an X-ray room, but it had been destroyed by enemy fire and was now useless.

For the rest, there were tiny shelters—mere

niches, some of them—on either side of the corridors. The corridors themselves, narrow as they
were, were in constant use. Men awaiting treatment lay on stretchers upon the ground, and often
there was barely room to pass by. Not that Geneviève wanted to pass by any of them; their plead-
ing eyes, their voices hoarse with pain, all touched
her tender heart.

Once she had met the staff, Geneviève began
her work. There were male nurses or orderlies,
and the tenderness of the lightly wounded for
those in serious straits was wonderful to see.
Geneviève helped in the operating room, where
Major Grauwin and Lieutenant Gindrey worked
for long hours. She changed dressings and fed
those who could not help themselves. She always
managed to find, in some mysterious way, some
small thing to ease the discomfort of the sufferers:
an extra cigarette, a smile that came from the
heart as well as from the lips, a bit of fruit. When
night came, she located an unused stretcher, dirty

and damp, in the operating room, and lay down upon it for her rest.

She had nothing but the clothes she had been wearing when she landed on the shelled airstrip, and one of the officers, distressed by her obvious need, said to her, "You'll be needing another shirt. Of course, mine will be a little large for *Mademoiselle,* but—" he shrugged, "both the shirt and I would be honored. . . ."

The word went around quickly that Geneviève needed clothing. Before many hours had gone by, she found herself the possessor of several shirts, prized cakes of soap, and even a few ounces of cologne. The men were eager to share their most cherished belongings with her, and Geneviève, realizing how much it meant to have a Frenchwoman in their midst, accepted them gracefully.

She was surrounded by thousands of men— desperate men, as their fighting in the next few weeks proved. Yet sometimes the thought sped through her mind that she could not have met more gentlemanly behavior in the salon of her uncle's chateau.

There was little time for such reflections. Two days after her arrival at Dien Bien Phu the Vietminh began shelling in earnest. The siege was on, that siege which the world was to watch for more than five weeks with anxiety and admiration.

She was pulled in all directions by her duties, as well as by her sympathies. The wounded poured into the little hospital in a steady stream, and sometimes in an overwhelming spate.

"*Mademoiselle,* will you take over here? I must see to the men in the Meo shelters."

"*Mademoiselle,* water, for the love of God!"

"*Mademoiselle,* my foot is hurting." The foot had been amputated, but Geneviève put some cotton under the ankle and the leg rested better.

"*Mademoiselle,* will you prepare this man for evacuation? The helicopter is coming in soon."

But the helicopter trip to Hanoi, which was for the most gravely wounded, had to be abandoned soon. The slow aircraft was too easy a target for the Viet shells. Several were blown to bits, and soon the helicopters no longer even attempted to make the trip to the besieged sector.

"What can we do now?" one young orderly asked, tossing his head in distress. "We haven't room for the *blessés* as it is, and if we can't even get any of them out . . . ." He did not need to finish his sentence, for the question was in all their minds. More and more wounded were arriving at the tiny hospital. Serious cases were being sent in from medical outposts by the battalion doctors. There was no place to put them.

For some time the lightly wounded had been placed in the shelters near the hospital, which had previously been occupied by some Meo tribesmen. It was dangerous, during the height of the shelling, to make the trip up the slippery stairs to the outside, and then across exposed ground to their entrance.

"We ought to dig a tunnel from the hospital to

those shelters," Geneviève said thoughtfully. She
had hesitated a moment before making the sug-
gestion, but because it was for her wounded she
brought it out.

Major Grauwin nodded in instant accord. "It
is certainly needed," he said, wiping the sweat
from his tired face. Geneviève thought that he
must have a terrible weight of responsibility upon
his shoulders—all these men here in the field
hospital, the supervision of their cases, as well as
the command of the battalion doctors scattered
in the various fortified outposts. And the operations! Although Lieutenant Gindrey was on his
feet at the operating table day and night, the
major did all the laparotomies, or abdominal
operations, and there were other serious operations that required his skill and experience.

She had been proud when, on her arrival,
Major Grauwin had put her in charge of a shelter
housing ten of the most serious cases. But Geneviève did not confine her nursing to them.

Although she gave them the best of care with the limited supplies on hand, she managed to find her way to other seriously wounded men, her calmness and serenity as soothing to them as some miraculous balm.

Nor did she come to them empty-handed, as a rule. Her thoughts were always with them. Many times, when she had finished the meal which she shared with the medical team, there would be a little something left over. Perhaps some jam, or a few crackers, or a bit of cheese. She never failed to collect these carefully, for she always knew just which of the men would be made happy by the treat she could offer.

Geneviève had been at Dien Bien Phu only a few days when one of the outposts, called Dominique, was attacked. It was fiercely defended, and the fighting and heavy shelling went on without interruption for three days and three nights. During the worst of it, the wires from the hospital's power plant were out, and the whole place was darkened. The wounded cried out in fear as well as in pain; there was confusion for a few moments until the orderlies could calm them.

When the lights went on again, they found that a shell had fallen on the sterilizer room. Men rushed there to dig out a stretcher buried in the earth. The wounded filled the corridors; there was not room for any more. Someone said, "They are packed in the trenches outside, waiting to get in."

Geneviève took her helmet and started out.

"*Mademoiselle,* you can't go out there!"

"But I am needed there," she answered quietly, and she hurried on to care for the men in the exposed areas.

There were wounded on stretchers under the beds and bunks, wounded under the table. A room which could hold fifteen stretched miraculously to hold twenty-five or more. Men cried out in pain, or moaned softly, or stared straight ahead with eyes that saw only their inner suffering. And everywhere, even in the most crowded places, there was Geneviève, adjusting a dressing, giving an injection, opening a can of fruit juice for a dry-lipped, silent man, talking to a scared boy, putting a cigarette between the lips of the man whose arm had just been amputated, feeding soup—spoonful by spoonful—to one whose jaws had been smashed and were now wired together so that he could not open them.

There was no pause in her busy days, and when night came she slept on a stretcher in the operating room. But seldom for long. There were always

too many among the wounded whom she found it
difficult to leave, and many more who needed her.
If only, she thought sometimes in despair, I could
divide myself into little pieces so that I could be
of service to more of them. For their uncomplain-
ing air and cheerful bravery haunted her more
than cries and groans would have.

Sometimes, as she straightened from her work,
Geneviève would stand for a moment, wondering
if this were all a dream—the noise of the guns,
the shouting of the men, the mud and the stench
and the pain. Surely it could not grow worse than
this! Surely it would end soon! But it did grow
worse, and it went on remorselessly for three days
and nights.

Yet never, in all this confusion of war, did she
lose her feeling of dedication. What else could
have given her the strength to stay on her feet, to
comfort the men who cried out in agony, to close
the eyes of those who had found release in death?
Whenever she entered one of the shelters, when-

ever she passed along one of the corridors jammed
with stretchers where there was scarcely foot-room
to pass, all eyes turned toward her, as if the men
saw in her the eternal promise of womanly com-
passion.

It was hard to be the only Frenchwoman on the
post. Yet it was rewarding, too. She could not help
but know how greatly she was treasured, even
though the men did not put this into words. The
eager clasp of weakened fingers, a whispered
"Merci, *mademoiselle*," were often her only out-
ward thanks, yet they carried a wealth of meaning
in their simplicity.

At last the attack on Dominique was over, for
Dominique had fallen. Geneviève saw that these
men were not discouraged by the defeat, only
angered, and more determined to fight it out
with the enemy than before. She was proud to be
working with a group of men like this. Their stub-
born optimism was wonderful to see.

It was catching, too, she thought, finding herself quite sure at times that they would yet win out against the Viets. And almost every night reinforcements were dropped in—men who had never made a parachute drop before but wanted to join their own outfits, to die with them if necessary.

Food and medical supplies were dropped by parachute, too, and although a full third of them landed on Viet territory or in a location too dangerous to send out men for them, the rest were always put to good use at once.

Geneviève had the pleasure of distributing many of the treats. There were sometimes fresh oranges and apples—incredibly welcome—and there were cans of fruit juice, or candy or cigarettes. She would take them eagerly and give them with an unerring instinct to the men who needed them most, sometimes going far afield to the distant shelters across the road in order to do it.

When things were a little calmer again, there were finally men to spare for the digging of the tunnel between the hospital and the shelters across the road which housed some of the wounded. It was all done in one night, with men working from both sides to do the digging, then roofed with logs, metal plates, and several feet of earth.

When it was finished and the shelters beyond had been made more habitable, Colonel Langlais came to make an inspection, and Geneviève was invited to come with him and his staff of officers. At one of the shelters, there was a curtain of clean parachute cloth hanging, and she was told to go in. There, like something out of the dreamed-of past, was a little cubicle furnished with cot, chair, and table. The walls and ceiling were covered with more parachute cloth, and the cot even had a coverlet of it.

When she turned, in surprise, and saw their faces, Geneviève knew that this was meant for her. It was unbelievable but true. It was one of the happiest moments of her life.

April brought great heat and more rains. Air in the underground hospital was completely lifeless, evil-smelling, and heavy. The rains brought rivulets of water to run down the walls and mingle with the earthen floors, until they were ankle deep in mud. Mushrooms and algae grew over the walls and the ceiling beams.

The dressings of the wounded were damp and could not be kept clean. Men perspired under their heavy casts and suffered from great running sores.

Yet despite the rains there was not enough water—water that they could use. None of the personnel were allowed to drink the precious stuff, and none were allowed any water in which to wash. Except Geneviève! She was given a basin of the precious liquid every day for her own use. The others tried to keep clean by using cotton and a little alcohol.

Water came from the river nearby, and even before this it had been a dangerous task for the water coolies to fetch it in large cans. Now, with the enemy closer and stronger than ever, it was almost impossible. Between the heavy fire, and the deep mud in the trenches, the trip which had once taken ten minutes, eventually took two hours, and then the water bearer would be exhausted from his exertions.

Many of the coolies were killed or wounded. Sometimes the orderlies made the trip when the need for water was really desperate, for they had to have water to keep the sterilizers going.

Many stretcher bearers were killed or wounded, too, and finally the military police took over this duty as well as the feeding of some of the wounded. The ambulances were destroyed, one by one, and the jeeps, too, until only a few trucks were left to try to bring in some of the wounded by night. Collecting the dropped supplies became more and more dangerous, and in one week more than two hundred coolies were lost in this alone.

There was no longer any place for the convalescent soldiers. Those who were on the way to recovery were sent back to their units—many of

them minus an arm or a leg or an eye—in order
to make room for the constantly arriving stream
of newly wounded men. They went without a mur-
mur. Some even begged for the chance to go, for
by this time many of them sensed that their fight
was to be a hopeless one, and they wanted to die
with their friends.

Those who were still well moved out of their
shelters into the trenches themselves, where they
dug holes or small recesses in which to crouch
during the bombardments. The wounded took
over their shelters, and those who could acted as
medical orderlies for their comrades. By this time
more than two thirds of the medical orderlies had
been put out of action.

Through all this, Geneviève remained her
sweet, refreshing self. Many a man, on the brink
of real despair, found his courage renewed at the
sight of her trim figure and softly smiling face
under the dark hair. It was such an innocent face,
yet one which had known sorrow and knew, too,

how to comfort the sorrowing. It was no surprise to Major Grauwin when he found, one day, that her little personal shelter had long since been occupied by wounded men, and that she was once more taking her rest wherever she could find a place to lie down.

One day in April, Geneviève was asked to lunch with General de Castries, the commanding officer. Her friends at the hospital wondered why she did not come back at once, for they knew her devotion. Yet when she returned, they saw the reason for her delay. There, pinned upon her blouse, were the *Légion d'Honneur* and the *Croix de Guerre* with a golden palm! No one deserved it more, they knew, but when they exclaimed over her, and wanted her to show her medals to the wounded, she shook her head.

"No," she said firmly. "I could not do that. Every one of those men deserves this more than I. I should be ashamed to have them see it."

She did not feel that way about another honor

which came her way, however. When the anniversary of the Kameroons came around—that day which is the one anniversary sacred to the Foreign Legion—she was summoned in the evening to the Command Post and was gone for most of the evening.

It was eleven when she came back to the muddy underground warren which had become her home. On her left sleeve she wore the green and black shield of the Legion. Almost at once one of the wounded men spotted it. "You're one of us now!"

he cried happily, and Geneviève said, "Yes, now I am more than ever one of you." She had been made an honorary Légionnaire, first Class, of the Thirteenth Demi-Brigade.

At once there was a wave of excitement in the dank, odorous rooms. One man told another, and he told a third. The sound swelled, as one after another joined in the joyful congratulations. It was a happy time for all.

This was the last happy note at Dien Bien Phu. With May, the rains increased, and the Viet bombardment grew heavier. The earth shook, and the water seeped in. Sometimes in mere trickles, sometimes in actual cascades. Shelters were weakened by the combination of moisture and vibration, and many of them collapsed. When the water became knee deep in them and in the trenches, the wounded men had to be placed in stretchers hung from the ceiling beams.

There were flies everywhere, and soon there were maggots. The maggots performed a good

office in eating bad flesh, yet they were frighten-
ingly repulsive, and no matter what the hospital
workers did, they could not get rid of them.

Every day Geneviève helped the major and
Sioni, an orderly, in the daily sorting out of the
wounded who lay in the passageway, awaiting
their fate. Some could be treated and sent back
to their units, some were moved along slowly
toward the operating room, some were past all
help and had to be removed to the morgue, an
area behind the hospital which had, by now,
become a vast field of the dead.

Despite the terrible wounds, there were always
some men whose courage and character stood out
above the others. Young Simon Marie was one
of these. Both his eyes had been destroyed by
a hand grenade, and he had lost three fingers on
one hand, and two on the other, so that his hands
were huge masses of dressings. Yet he was always
cheerful, and even played, after a fashion, on a
little harmonica which the major gave him, to

entertain his fellow patients. And he was only eighteen!

He always brightened when Geneviève came to see him, or brought him a can of fruit juice to drink, or a cigarette to smoke. "We shall have a promenade together when we get to Hanoi, *mademoiselle*," he would say with an air of certainty. Geneviève tried hard to keep the depression from her voice when she replied, "Of course, we will, Simon Marie."

For it was becoming more and more evident that Hanoi was only a dream in the future. She wondered if any of them would ever see it again.

The last few days were a nightmare that none of those who survived will ever forget. Endless shelling, endless streams of wounded, no supplies, no stretcher bearers. Nothing but the patience of the wounded and the miraculous strength of those who served them. There was no sleep for anyone.

Now only the walking wounded could come to the hospital, and at the end they told Geneviève that they had been sent on by the Viets. The conquering horde was closing in quickly, and did not want to be bothered by these men. Now the French troops heard, above the sounds of the bombardment, the explosions as they destroyed their own ammunition depots, their own arms and equipment. There was nothing to look forward to but capture—then death or an internment camp.

The wounded were piled one upon the other in the rooms and were wedged tight in the passages. Those who died, simply sank deeper into the mud. It was horrible, unbelievable. But through it all, Geneviève moved, distributing the last of the provisions, tireless in her efforts to help and comfort, and her sweet voice fell upon the men's ears like a blessing. Her own shelter was crammed with serious cases. Her uniform was stained with mud and blood. She had had no sleep for two days when the Viets took over.

The hospital personnel were ordered out. Their hearts sank as they climbed the slippery steps to the open air. What lay in store for them after this? Even more terrible was the question which confronted them all: What would become of their wounded? Who would care for them?

It was strange to see a calm blue sky. Now that the guns had ceased firing, the silence was overpowering. In a daze, Geneviève followed Major Grauwin down to the bridge, across the river. They were prisoners now and did not know what lay ahead. But Geneviève felt that she would rather have died with her wounded than leave them like this.

Suddenly a Viet appeared before them. He spoke in French, "Go back to the hospital, and look after your wounded. This is an order from the high command of our army."

The major wheeled about eagerly, his face alight. And Geneviève went with him, almost running to keep up with his long strides. "Oh, I'm so *glad*," was all she could say. But her whole heart was in it.

Frontier Nurse

MARY BRECKENRIDGE

Few people are able to foretell their own lives in any way, or to guess what small happening may turn their energies and interests into new channels. In the early years of her life, Mary Breckenridge longed for a life of adventure and exploration. Adventure was to be hers, indeed, but her exploration took the form of exploring new ways of improving nursing service in isolated rural areas, and in the development of nursing-midwife training in this country.

Her father was our minister to Russia in the days of the czars, and it was in St. Petersburg, now Leningrad, that her younger brother was born. A Russian midwife brought him into the world, and since Mary Breckenridge was thirteen at the time this made quite an impression on her. She realized, from that time, that a doctor was not always necessarily present at the birth of a child.

Her experiences were varied in her childhood and young womanhood. Life in a country as sophisticated, and yet as crude, as czarist Russia, with French and German governesses, was followed by school in Switzerland. There were vacations on the French Riviera, and later, when her family had returned to the United States, there was a period in Washington, D. C., while her father served in Congress. There were visits to Tennessee, and to a cotton plantation in Arkansas where her aunts and uncles lived. And there was her beloved summer home, "The Brackens," in Canada.

She learned to ride a horse early, and she learned to ride bareback. This was to be of great use to her later. She learned to make-do with conditions as they were without complaint and to accept physical hardship almost with pleasure. These things were, after all, adventure.

Mary Breckenridge had always loved children, but she had never dreamed of being a nurse. It was natural for her to marry, natural to hope for children of her own. When she was left a young widow, she felt doubly bereft. But it was not until she sat by the bedside of a typhoid-stricken child, in North Carolina, where she was visiting, that her thoughts for the future began to take definite form.

She felt helpless in the face of disease and angry at her own helplessness. It was then that she decided to take nurse's training, and, in her decisive way, she set about it as soon as she could.

But her education had not been the normal one for an American girl, and when she entered St. Luke's Hospital she found that she had to be tutored in arithmetic, or she might have given the wrong dosages to her patients!

For three years she trained at St. Luke's, her greatest interest always centered on the sick babies. The hours were incredibly long, and conditions sometimes difficult, but she did not miss a single day.

For a while after that, it might have seemed to an onlooker that she had forgotten her desire to care for sick children, for she spent the year following her graduation in caring for her mother who was ill. Then, marrying for a second time, she devoted herself to her son, Breckenridge, whom she called "Breckie."

Breckie had a little sister who did not live for more than a few hours, and this was a great sorrow to Mary. Then, when Breckie died at the age of four, Mary Breckenridge turned once more for consolation to her old ambition.

World War I was drawing to a close when she volunteered for Red Cross service in France, but there was to be a hectic interlude in this country before she could sail. In the flu epidemic Washington was badly hit and Mary Breckenridge, as a qualified nurse, went into action at once. People were stricken by the thousands, and there were not nearly enough doctors or nurses to care for all the ill people, so each nurse had command of a corps of civilian volunteer aides, who did wonderful work under their trained leaders.

By the time her papers came through for France, the Armistice had been declared, and the Red Cross was canceling the sailings of its personnel. She was so anxious to get to France to work with the children there, that she obtained her release from the Red Cross and volunteered for the American Committee for Devastated France.

The French name for this committee had the initials C-A-R-D, and the people who worked with the committee were often called "Cards" for convenience and brevity. They were a hardworking group, earnest and efficient and eager to help the people of the devastated areas to return to their homes and farms and to a normal life again.

Everything was needed—food, clothing, supplies, buildings. One important need was for seeds so that the farmers could sow their first crops after the war. There were no civilian doctors in the sector where Mrs. Breckenridge worked, for they had not yet returned, but there were a few military doctors. Almost at once, under difficult conditions where everything had to be improvised, she began her nursing service.

The children were pathetic, they were so undersized and undernourished. Supplies were scarce, and milch cows almost nonexistent. She spoke, in one of her letters home, of the tragic conditions in many of the families, and she said, "If I could give a goat right now to every family that has a baby, I think we could go far toward saving many that are dying. There is much grippe and pneumonia among them and they have no powers of resistance. I wish I had a thousand goats right now. I wish I had fifty."

Her fervent wish bore immediate fruit. Members of her family gave goats and started goat funds. A goat cost twenty dollars, and soon there was enough money to order a number of them. They came from the Pyrenees by the train carload, each group with its own goatherd to do the feeding and milking on the long trip north.

The young children and babies of her sector interested Mrs. Breckenridge the most, and caught at her heartstrings with their tiny hands. So many mothers were undernourished that they were unable to nurse their babies, and the death rate was very high. In the few places where there was a free distribution of milk, there was no instruction given on the care of children, and no follow-up. Mrs. Breckenridge saw at once that what was needed in France was a good public

health or visiting nurse service. But such women would have to be trained nurses first.

It was here that she discovered how lacking France was in trained nurses. There were trained midwives, but trained nurses were extremely scarce. With graduates of one of the good nursing schools, she was able to establish a visiting public health nurse service in quite a large area, but when she tried to go further, she found that there would first have to be good training schools for nurses, and this was an impossibility because the state employees of the hospitals refused to permit it.

Yet she had the satisfaction of knowing that what she had done in her sector had brought health and renewed energy to many, and that many lives had been saved through her efforts.

With this postwar work behind her, she began to think of the future. There were children in her own country, she knew, who faced life under almost as great difficulties as the French children in the devastated area. There were places where whole sections of our population had no doctor within miles, no nurses at all, and where life was an unceasing struggle for simple survival.

Because her ancestors had come to Kentucky in its earliest days, because her own father had been born there, her thoughts turned naturally to the mountain people of that state. Hadn't she always loved mountain country better than any other kind? And did she not know, from experience, the courtesy and hospitality of these people? She knew, too, how desperately they were in need of the kind of nursing service she wanted to give them.

Now she spent a year at Columbia University in a course on public health nursing and allied subjects, and then a summer on horse and muleback, riding through that part of Kentucky where she hoped to settle. She chose an area that was completely inaccessible by rail or car, where there were no roads, and where even the trails were sometimes hard to find.

She visited many families, fording rivers and following creeks, sleeping wherever dark found her, sharing the simple meals of the mountaineers. She met the native midwives who brought the babies into the world. And always she was observing, estimating, planning.

There have been few projects as thoroughly thought about, planned for, and executed as Mary Breckenridge's Frontier Nursing Service, as it was to become known. If she had allowed herself to be swayed by emotion alone, she might have gone into the work only half prepared, without proper training, without sufficient backing, without a vision of the needs that the future would bring. Most important of all, perhaps, she had the realization of what such a service, carefully carried out *and recorded,* could mean to other services in other isolated areas.

With this in mind, she went to England, for it was in England that there was opportunity for a trained nurse to get instruction in midwifery. "In France," as she says in her book, *Wide Neighborhoods,* "midwives were not nurses. In America, nurses were not midwives. In England trained women were both nurses and midwives."

She entered the British Hospital for Mothers and Babies, where the course for trained nurses lasted four months. She writes that the hospital was exceedingly damp, and says, in her delightful fashion, that it was the " . . . dampest place in the world, short of a frog pond." For four months she was constantly and tormentingly *cold*—so cold that when she received permission to use the gas heater in her room, she burned a hole in one of her legs without noticing it!

Her next step was a most sensible one. She went to Scotland to study the nursing service there in the highlands, and on the scattered islands of the Hebrides. This service, she realized, had many of the problems which she would be meeting in her own Frontier Nursing Service, and she found their system well worth studying. She learned several important things here: that local committees were best when run by local, interested people; how to lodge the nurses; how to transport the nurses to the patients.

Next came postgraduate work in midwifery in London, and finally, early in 1925, she came back to Kentucky, where she was to carry on her chosen work. There was a great deal of labor involved in the organization of this project, which was to cover a territory in which fifteen thousand people lived without the services of a doctor. And, in order to understand just how well her service would be functioning, she had to have some sort of statistics with which to compare.

She engaged Miss Bertram Ireland (who, surprisingly, came from Scotland!) to make a survey of births and deaths in the area. This meant interviewing from house to house, from farm to farm in the mountains. They found, almost at once, that mountain people were plagued by parasites, and that most mountain babies had dysentery. There were flies everywhere in the hot months, and sanitation was nonexistent. The creeks and rivers were polluted, and typhoid fever was all too common.

While Miss Ireland and her helpers were making their survey, Mary Breckenridge was more than busy herself. She traveled about the United States, interesting many of her influential friends in her new undertaking, and the first regional committees had their start then. These committees were to aid in the support of the project.

As time went on, more and more groups heard of her work and agreed to support it. Individuals gave of their time and money, church organizations helped maintain it, and a national sorority established a social service in connection with the Frontier Nursing Service.

The start of Hyden Hospital was made at this time, in the only vacant house in the little town of Hyden. It was a ramshackle house with no facilities, and quite small. But it was a beginning. Besides, it had a clean well and a barn for the horses. This was important, for there was only one way for the nurses to reach their patients— on horseback. They carried their nursing and midwifery supplies in specially designed saddlebags.

The first supplies were ordered and began to come in: typhoid serum and diphtheria toxin-antitoxin headed the list of drugs. There were croup kettles and hypodermic needles, baby scales, and even fish kettles for boiling supplies. All these had to be brought in laboriously from the nearest railroad spur, while the river was low enough to be forded.

There were two nurse-midwives to start the service. Mary Breckenridge herself was in the saddle all day, and then up half the night writing orders and letters on an old typewriter. But the Frontier Nursing Service, which was to become nationally and internationally known, had begun.

That same summer and fall the first nursing

center was built. It was located on a site which Mrs. Breckenridge had found two years before on her first trip through the area, and which had appealed to her so greatly that she planned to live there herself. That was where Wendover, her home, was constructed.

Between 1927 and 1930 the six outpost nursing centers were built and staffed. Each was so located that the nurses in any one of them served about one thousand people within a radius of five miles. There were usually two nurse-midwives at each center, where there was not only a comfortable house for them, but a dispensary for treating ambulatory patients as well. There was a housekeeper to keep the nurses from being overburdened with work, but even so there was more than enough to do, for the nurses usually oversaw the building operations, gardened, and saw to the care of the "property," as mountain people called the livestock.

With the centers in operation, the first couriers

came into the picture—young girls who spent
several months at a time in the Frontier Nursing
Service as volunteers. They had to be strong and
healthy, excellent horsewomen who could not
only ride well but who could tend the horses and
care for the mounts of the nurses and themselves
when the animals were sick. They brought supplies to the centers from the hospital or the railroad; they sometimes helped the nurses on their
rounds, and often they brought in a sick child to
the hospital at Hyden.

Many of the accident cases among children
were terrible burns, and there were usually little
girls, whose dresses had caught fire when they
stood too near the hearth. It was a common frontier occurrence, although a sad one, for when our
ancestors first discarded their wool and linsey-
woolsey clothing for cotton there were the same
sad accidents: many children killed or scarred
for life. One thing that Mary Breckenridge
succeeded in doing was persuading the parents of

little girls to put them into overalls and to screen the fires.

Mrs. Breckenridge herself was the victim of a serious accident, and it happened at a time when the Frontier Nursing Service was desperately in need of her work. Only a few days after her staff had presented her with a handsome, spirited horse, he was frightened by the flapping of her cape-raincoat, and he bolted. When she knew she could no longer cling to the saddle with her knees, she threw herself off.

She might easily have been killed, but the results of the runaway were bad enough—she had a broken back. Then came months on a Bradford frame, many more months in a steel brace. It was during this time of suffering and worry that she learned how well she had planned and organized, how truly devoted her friends and the friends of the Service were. She was not allowed to make her usual rounds by horseback for seventeen months, but when she finally did so, the welcome she received everywhere told her how needed and appreciated the Frontier Nursing Service was, and how much its director was loved by the people she served.

Nowadays the Service is no longer completely dependent upon horses and mules, as it was in its early days. There are nineteen jeeps, a truck, and a station-wagon ambulance. But there are still horses, too, for roads have not been built in many places where the Frontier Nursing Service must venture. The hospital has grown, and the people of the district no longer have to be coaxed by the nurses to have preventive injections or to call for help in time of sickness. They speak of the nurses as "our nurses" and of Mary Breckenridge as "our Director."

There have been modernizations in many fields, but there is still the same unselfish desire to help behind everything that the Frontier Nursing Service does. Mrs. Roger K. Rogan, wife of a trustee, spoke truly when she said of it that

" . . . utilitarian things seemed to be done with spiritual insight."

People are still very poor in the mountain section of Kentucky which the Frontier Nursing Service serves, but they are not as poor as they were when the FNS was started. In those days the midwifery fee was five dollars, but there was seldom that much money available. The Service took many things in exchange for nursing care: quilted "kivers" and split-bottomed chairs, labor at the various centers, or food if there was a surplus.

There have been other rewards for those who have given this extraordinary service; rewards which could not possibly be thought of in terms of money. Perhaps a little crippled boy expressed this best, when he returned from a long stay at a hospital "outside" to which Frontier Nursing Service had sent him for treatment. He said, in his soft mountain speech, "I've most forgot what it feels like to be a-hurtin'."

Those who have stopped "a-hurtin'," and those whose children have been brought safely into the world by the nurse-midwives of the Frontier Nursing Service, those who have been saved from the choking death of diphtheria or the coughing death of tuberculosis—all these and many others owe much to the vision and foresight and determination of a woman who wanted to help—their friend, Mary Breckenridge.

When she was a girl she longed for a life of exploration and adventure. She has had more adventure than most people even dream of. As for exploration—she has explored many avenues of service to humanity, and she has found rich treasures of admiration and love.

Settlement Nurse

LILLIAN WALD

"Favey!" Lillian's clear voice rang out, and she clasped her hands in joy.

"Do you like it?" her grandfather asked, beaming at her fondly. But one look at her face had told him that.

"It's the most beautiful dollhouse in the whole wide world! Oh, Favey!" and she flung her arms around his neck. "You are so good to me!"

Favey—that was the Wald children's name for
their Grandfather Schwarz—said, "Look inside."

She darted through the little door. "Real doll
furniture!" she breathed. "And a couch—it's big
enough for me. . . . I can put all my dolls to sleep
on it. And a stove! Oh, oh!"

"You can cook on it. Will you make pancakes
for me?"

"Every day," Lillian promised.

When she had looked her fill he led her back
along the flower-bordered path to the big house.
"You do such nice things!" Lillian cried, her eyes
shining. "You're always giving me presents, and
Julie and Alfred and Gus, too, of course. Ponies
. . . Kitty is my favorite, I'll never let her die—and
ice cream parties, and trips to the theatre. And
you tell us stories . . . Favey, would you tell me
another story right now? Let's go up on the porch
and you tell me about when you were a little boy
in Germany."

They settled themselves on the wide veranda

and Lillian gave a wriggle of contentment. She was really the luckiest little girl in the country, she thought. With a grandfather like Favey, and Uncle Samuel, who came to visit and brought trunks full of books and read to them. With her gentle father, who did so many kind things, and her beautiful mother, who took her to concerts and plays and the opera and to hear great speakers as well as for rides in the carriage.

"Now that you have the dollhouse," Favey was saying, "I have another idea."

"What is it? Tell me, tell me!"

"Not yet," he smiled, teasing her. "I must work it out. But it will come soon. I think you will like my idea."

It wasn't too long before she found out what it was to be . . . a bowling alley under the arbor. A bowling alley of their very own. Favey had thought of a way to make the balls come back to the bowler, and all the neighborhood children came to play with her and her sister and brothers.

One day, however, a ball bounced out of the trough and hit Lillian on the head. Favey was distracted! He was afraid she had been badly injured and would not forgive himself. Even when the doctor said she was not seriously harmed, he took her on his lap and told her stories to make her forget . . . and promised her another pony.

That was why, in later years, Lillian Wald would say that she was a spoiled child. But it was a happy household, and the happy things that took place in her childhood helped to form her understanding and sympathetic character. She knew what it meant to be joyous and privileged, and she wanted that for other people.

She had been born in Cincinnati, but her father's business took him to Rochester, New York, and it was there that most of her childhood and young womanhood were spent. She was ready for Vassar at sixteen, but the president of the college thought she should wait another year before entering because she was so young. She had been to private schools and she was not sure what she wanted to do, but she knew that she wanted to do *something* while she waited to go to college. Life wasn't all parties and dancing and a gay social whirl. But what could she do?

Lillian's older sister Julia got married in the meantime and was expecting a baby. Lillian went to visit her and met her sister's nurse, a young woman who had studied at Bellevue. Lillian had never talked to a nurse before and was fascinated by the stories of her training and experience that the young woman told. It opened up a whole new world to her, a world she was determined to enter.

Her family tried to change her mind. It would mean hardship and discipline, and no one had tried to discipline Lillian before. She was gentle and sweet, but she was firm. She was going to be a nurse . . . and her family gave in, as they always had.

She chose the New York Hospital for her training. Miss Irene Sutliffe, who became famous herself, was in charge and showed the young, eager-eyed woman through. Lillian was horrified to see a young boy's leg suspended from an apparatus, feeling sure he must be in dreadful pain. "Not at all," Miss Sutliffe said. "He's the hero of the ward. And if you come in, you and he will have great fun together."

Hospital life was new and strange and there were more rules and regulations in one day than she had met with in her entire life. One night, soon after her arrival, she was sent to the basement on an errand and heard shrieks coming from a cell. She peered in and saw an old man with wild eyes. "Nobody's given me anything to eat," he cried, when she asked what was the matter. "I'm starving!"

Lillian thought that was dreadful and rushed to find someone in authority. But no one was in and she told the elevator boy her trouble. He said that the nurse from the diet kitchen left the keys with him when she went away and he handed them over to her. "Help yourself," he said.

She did, and brought the man in the cell all kinds of delicacies that she found in the refrigerator reserved for special patients. Next morning she went to Miss Sutliffe and said heatedly that it was a shame any patient in the hospital had to starve. Miss Sutliffe was a wise and understanding woman. Instead of scolding the young student nurse she said, "It was irregular, Miss Wald. He was drunk and unconscious when he was brought in and could not be fed. You should have asked permission to go to the diet kitchen. But personally I am glad you fed the old man."

Lillian Wald found it hard to go into the operating room. But here, too, Miss Sutliffe was wise. When one of Lillian's patients was due for an operation, her superior said, "If you went with her, I think she would feel happier." That made a difference. It didn't help to feel pity and then shrink away. The pity you felt mattered only if you did something about it. She could go to the operating room because her patient needed her.

Her nurse's training was only eighteen months long, and after that she became a nurse at the Juvenile Asylum, but she saw so much that made her unhappy there that she left after a year. This was not the place for her, and she felt she could do more for children some other way. She did not know enough yet. She would study to be a doctor.

She went to the Women's Medical College. There were very few women doctors; it was only forty years since Elizabeth Blackwell had blazed the way by receiving the first medical degree given a woman. Lillian studied hard, she learned to face pain and disease and all the unpleasant things that can happen to people. One evening she was asked to go down to the College Settlement on Henry Street to show a group of women how to do home nursing. This was part of her training. She had never been in the poor section of the city.

In the midst of her demonstration showing how to fold a sheet, a child rushed in, asking for help for her mother who was desperately ill. Lillian followed her through the dark streets and up the rotting stairway to the dank two rooms where seven people were living. What she found there opened her eyes to conditions which she had only vaguely heard about. While she bathed the sick woman and gave her comfort, and calmed the weeping child, her eyes took in the pitiful conditions, and her heart cried out to do something about them.

This was not just one case in a great city—this

was one case with thousands like it. There were
so many unfortunate people in the city who
needed help . . . her hospital training and her
training to be a doctor made her aware of that.
But she could not wait to become a doctor. She
must begin at once! She would bring nursing right
to the homes that needed it. When she went down
the stairway in the early morning her mind was
made up. She knew what her life work was to be.

Her first fellow worker was a friend, Mary
Brewster, who had also graduated from New
York Hospital as a nurse. They found a small
apartment on Jefferson Street, up five flights—
but it had a bathroom—and let it be known in the
neighborhood that they were there to help.

At first the calls were slow in coming in. People
were distrustful. They could not believe that these
young women really meant what they said. Lillian
Wald and her friend waited . . . they were good
neighbors and friendly and interested. Finally an
elderly man came to see them. "I came up here

because they said here was some ladies who would listen," he said. And that was the beginning. For they not only listened—they helped.

It was a year when there was a great depression. Thousands were out of work; they had little money, little food, and illness was everywhere.

The two nurses found children with eye diseases and vermin bites. They found typhoid and pneumonia. There were a crippled child and her mother living on dry crusts of bread. There was a family which had only ten dollars a month. Six of those dollars were paid for rent. "They slept," wrote Miss Wald in one of her endless reports, "on rags in an unlighted room." There were children who had no shoes and could not go to the country, and others so naked they had to be clothed before they could be sent to a sanatorium.

Newspapers offered tickets for free ice at ice depots and tickets for fresh air excursions, and the two nurses gave these away. They enlisted the help of hospitals and various charities. But there

was never enough. Lillian Wald never called these
people "the poor"; she had too great sympathy
for that. She said they were the unfortunates, and
they must be helped. Some who needed help
would not take it. She told of one proud young
Russian who refused money until she got a friend
of hers to ask him to tutor her son so that he
could be paid.

Wherever they went they saw things that needed
to be done and needed to be changed. Two years
before the Health Commissioner of New York
launched his own anti-tuberculosis campaign,
Lillian Wald had a long list of patients for the
Board of Health to take on. She tried not only to
nurse the sick but to discover what made them
sick and what could be done to prevent it. On less
than a hundred dollars a month—which came out
of her own, and Miss Brewster's, private income—
she managed to buy eggs and milk, prescriptions,
train fare for a boy to go to Saranac, money to fix
someone's spectacles, money for rent.

Taking care of people in their own homes was really the beginning of the visiting nurses associations which spread all over the world. Other things that Lillian Wald did were also the beginings of other reforms. When she found a grocery store, for instance, that was not clean, she would ask the grocer to put netting over the cheese and fruit. When she treated children for scalp ailments, she started the idea of having school nurses. When she discovered that many of the immigrant mothers did not know how to cook or serve American foods, she gave lessons in preparing simple dishes that were not expensive and were nourishing for children.

She used tact and firmness to get people over their fear of doctors and hospitals. She kept in touch with her patients after they were well, and tried to see that they had work and proper living conditions. When things went wrong, or she found bad practices, she could be stern. The people began to call her "She-who-must-be-obeyed." And one Chinese man, knowing of her many good deeds, said she was "Heavenly lady number one."

Little by little the neighbors and their friends came to rely on her and Miss Brewster. The work grew—soon there were four nurses instead of two. People brought their problems to her, or sometimes they just came to chat or for a visit. They brought her little gifts to show their appreciation, and she treasured these. After a time there wasn't room in the apartment. They had so many friends, so many patients, so many others needing help, and so many wanting to visit, that they had to have a bigger place. Miss Wald found a solid three-story house that, as a friend of hers said, " . . . seemed to have an open and serene expression and to be utterly charming," and they bought it. It had a little garden at the rear. And this was the beginning of the Henry Street Settlement.

It was surprising how much happened in that one house. In the course of time 250 nurses would

go out in a single day to visit 1,300 patients and care for people of twenty-five different nationalities. These young women in blue, whom Miss Wald had so carefully chosen, made their countless rounds among the people who were ill but who would never have gone to a hospital. Sometimes the nurses had a hard time finding the address of the ill person; even the policeman on the beat was not sure.

The nurses did as much work as several hospitals . . . and no call, whether it came by mail or

telephone or messenger, was ever refused. The
nurses had the spirit of an army, and nothing
diverted them. On salaries of thirty dollars a week,
or less—some were volunteers and accepted no
salary at all—they did a wonderful work. Nor was
their work over when they had cared for the sick.
They came back to the Settlement House and, as
often as not, conducted classes in nursing care,
hygiene, cooking, or English. They were devoted
young women, always inspired by the example of
Lillian Wald and encouraged by her appreciation
and enthusiasm.

Classes were held in all kinds of subjects, there
were recreation rooms for children and adults,
there was a constant stream of people coming for
advice and help. And in the heart of the house,
which was Miss Wald's office, new ideas sprang
to life and were put into action.

Lillian Wald had a constant concern for children and their welfare, and for years she had been
distressed by child labor. More than that, as she

often pointed out, no one seemed to know, or care, how many children were born and died, how many were in jails or almshouses. One morning she decided to act. The Federal government *must* become concerned about the children of the United States.

It took her years to get action, but she did not give up until she had written and spoken and lectured and worked, had brought pressure to bear in high places, and had the aid of influential people. In due course the Children's Bureau was formed, an agency to take care of all these problems concerning children. Everyone wanted Lillian Wald to be its head, but she refused. Now that it was a fact, she had other work to do.

She was always busy, but never too busy to listen to the story of someone in trouble, someone needing help or advice. She made the work of the Henry Street Settlement known far and wide, so that money came in for at least *some* of the things she was always wanting to do.

There were all kinds of clubs formed at Henry Street for boys and girls, but Miss Wald's favorite was the American Heroes' Club, which was the very first one. It was made up of boys who had not been friends of the Settlement at first and whom she had had to win over. These boys, who had made nuisances of themselves when the Settlement first came to Henry Street, grew to be its most loyal supporters. When a campaign for a new club building, with gymnasium, library, reading room, game rooms, and meeting rooms was started, some of the club members who were employed walked to their work so that they could give their carfare to the fund. Many of those boys later had fine careers, or fought for their country, or were successful businessmen. And many of them came back to tell her of their success and to help her in her work.

She liked the clubs to manage themselves as freely as possible. Only once did she interfere and that was when a group decided not to accept a

Chinese boy who wanted to come in. She told them that if they didn't admit him they could not meet at the Settlement, and then she invited a Chinese woman doctor who spoke English fluently to come and give a talk about her native country. The club members had never realized what a wonderful culture other nations had, and the attractive Chinese doctor impressed them. They changed their minds, and the Chinese boy eventually became one of their most popular members. It was one of Lillian Wald's most cherished victories.

She liked to tell stories on herself . . . and they always proved a point to her listeners. One time, she recalled, when she was entertaining some important visitors, a delegation of fish peddlers called on her to ask her help. She wanted to know if her visitors could listen in, but they said no. "They wouldn't know what we were talking about," the men said. "But you would. Why, you even *feel* like a fish peddler!"

She "felt like" all people, whatever their work or their station in life, if they had problems or needed help. That was the secret of her success.

If boys got into trouble, as they did with neighbors or city policemen, and were brought to court, Miss Wald was their friend. If necessary she talked to them or found work for them. She gave them discipline, but she also gave them affection and understanding . . . and they straightened out. They had to, for she expected it of them. She never gave up a boy in trouble.

Lillian Wald brought musicians, speakers, dancers, and singers to the House, so that her neighbors could enjoy them. She opened doors to worlds of art and music that had been closed till then; she broadened their horizons, made them aware of other fields. Festivals and holidays were celebrated with pageants and song, and the neighbors were always part of it. Life grew richer because of her and her determination that their days should not have only work and worry.

Out of this grew the Henry Street Playhouse, which some of her wealthy friends made possible. Now they could put on plays and pantomimes and pageants for adults and children. Actors famous the world over played at Henry Street. Concert artists sang for them. The Settlement House people were enriched and uplifted.

A never-ending stream of good things came out of Henry Street. Lillian Wald was vitally concerned with improving children's conditions; new housing and sanitation; suffrage; sweatshops. As a "spoiled child," she had known how to wind her family around her finger. As a woman she knew how to present her facts and figures to people in high places and make them see what needed to be done—with new laws or with money. Because of her great heart and her fine mind, she brought health and happiness to thousands of people; she bettered the living conditions of millions; she fought for justice wherever it was needed.

Her life was full to overflowing, yet she always had time for her friends. And her friends ranged from the Prime Minister of England and his daughter to the janitress of an apartment house; from a peddler on the street corner to one of the wealthiest men in New York City.

The bigger the Settlement House grew, the more work she had, and the more work she had, the more she undertook. When doctors finally told her that she must rest, she found it very hard, but she did retire to a lovely old house she had bought in Connecticut called House-on-the-Pond. There she watched the changing seasons and the birds and her garden; there people came to see her— the great and the near-great; Jane Addams of Hull House and Mrs. Roosevelt; some of her American Heroes boys and the young women on the nursing staff. There she wrote and planned what she would do when she was well. For there was still so much to do!

When she died, more than three thousand

people came to the Henry Street house that had been her home for forty years. Other thousands jammed Carnegie Hall where a memorial service was held. Everyone mourned her, the famous men and women whose hearts and pocketbooks had opened to her needs; the boy who had walked four miles to save her a two-cent stamp; the woman who had found new hope because of Lillian Wald's advice; the children who were plump and rosy now after having had tuberculosis; the corner greengrocer and the uptown matron . . . all came to pay her honor, knowing that although she was dead she would live forever in the hearts of those who had loved her, and that the work she had begun would never die.

The Most Thrilling Thing

LORA WOOD HUGHES

"I want to make people well, too," Lora Wood told her idol, Ike, the family's cow hand. She greatly admired her mother, who was always in demand when any neighbor was sick.

Ike looked at her fondly. "You will, Doc, you will," he told her. "Doc" was his name for her always, and she was very proud of it. She did not aim to be a doctor, however; she had her heart

191

set on being a nurse. When Ike had a bad cold in his chest, Lora's mother let her make the mustard plaster to go on it, and when he came into the kitchen the next morning with a huge blister, she was allowed to prick it with a big darning needle her father heated for her.

She nursed the animals, there on their Kansas prairie farm, and one time she had the thrilling experience of saving a neighbor's finger tip. He was whetting his scythe when the blade slipped and the finger tip was all but severed. "Put it back on!" Lora cried, whipping out her new handkerchief to bind it tight. Then she poured turpentine on it, for that was what she had seen her mother do for the family dog when he got his foot caught in a mowing machine. The treatment was rough and painful, but it worked. The finger was saved.

She had many such adventures while she was still a child. There was the time an old hill-woman, living nearby, flipped hot ashes from her pipe into her eyes. Lora's mother, when she heard

of it, made a jug of strong, strained tea and sent
Lora over to keep the burned and inflamed eyes
of the old woman covered with wet tea com-
presses. Every fifteen minutes for the entire afternoon, she changed the wet packs, and by evening she had the satisfaction of seeing the eyes
almost normal, with the swelling greatly reduced.

When a doctor finally moved into the neighborhood, she impressed him by her reasoning, and
he lent her medical books and charts to read.

Their stone house in Kansas was comfortable,
and when they went into the nearby town for
the winter, her father was always busy as a builder.
But he had an itching foot, and so, when she was
about to enter her teens, they moved to California.
It was in the midst of a real-estate boom. They
were all sure they would make a fortune there.
The ranch was sold, the furniture shipped ahead,
and the family went on by emigrant train.

They lived in a tent house at first, but an unex-
pected storm came raging out of the Sierra Madre

Mountains, and they lost almost everything they owned. For days after they had moved in with an aunt, the children went back to the place where they had lived, searching for their scattered belongings. They were lucky to be alive.

Good luck was not to be with them long, however. They were no sooner settled again than all six of the Wood children came down with scarlet fever. Lora was the first one back on her feet, and with the true spirit of a devoted nurse she forgot her own feelings in helping to nurse the others. But even with her help, there was nothing they could do to save the baby.

Now they were poor, and the days of struggle began. For most of her life, Lora was to know real struggle. It seems strange now that it should have been so difficult for her to realize her ambition of becoming a nurse, but in the last portion of the nineteenth century there were many obstacles to overcome if one lived in California and was poor besides.

When Lora had finished high school, she knew what she wanted to do, but there seemed no way of doing it. The first nurse's training schools had been established in New York and Boston almost twenty years before, but west of Chicago there were few places where a girl could be trained.

She had consulted a few doctors concerning her problem, and they had told her she would be wise to go to any hospital which would take her in, get training as a practical nurse, and drop all idea of becoming a registered nurse. But Lora had other ideas, and she was not one to drop them easily. She wanted to be a trained nurse; she wanted her diploma. But how to get it?

When her family left for Montana to help run a sheep ranch, Lora stayed behind in Los Angeles. She married a man whom she had known for some time, and he helped her get work at a hospital. She took a few months' training in City Hospital, and then she was sent out as a district nurse and investigator by Associated Charities.

There was no pay for her hard work but plenty of experience, and Lora welcomed experience.

Then came a depression. Lora's husband lost his job, and that meant that she could not afford to keep on with her work, no matter how interesting it might be. She gave up her nursing and did piece work in a cannery, while her husband's health failed steadily. To make matters worse, her only child was born at this time and did not live long. When the baby died, Lora's husband, who had always traveled a great deal before he married, decided to go on a long sea voyage. He died before she could see him again.

Lora was restless. She heard of the terrible typhoid epidemic in Honolulu and decided to become an Army nurse so that she could go out and nurse the soldiers there. But when she made inquiries, she discovered that the unit of Army nurses was not to be sent out for some time, so she went as a civilian nurse, paying her own fare.

She found conditions much worse than she had

expected. When she got to the hospital, she told
Major Wood (later Major General Wood) that
she wanted to enlist right away in order to help.
"There is no enlistment for nurses as yet," he told
her. "You will have to go in under contract, at
forty dollars a month and two rations a day."

As soon as she had signed the contract she was
assigned to a bungalow which was in the charge
of a medical student. The moment she entered
the door, she was appalled at what she saw—
and smelled! Cots were jammed so close together
that there was scarcely room to move. The boys
upon the cots were all very, very sick.

When young Poole, the medical student,
learned that she was a nurse and wanted to help,
he could hardly believe it.

"How soon can you be ready?" he asked.

"Give me an apron. I'm ready now," she
answered.

This was the answer Lora gave to all who
needed her during her long career of nursing. She

did not wait for arrangements to be made nor stipulate that she must have things a certain way before she would work. She never asked for anything for herself. She was always "ready now."

In the weeks that followed, Lora's heart was wrung with pity almost constantly. The suffering of the boys was dreadful, and conditions were unbelievably bad. As one of her patients cried, "We're rotting here like rats in an alley!"

It took time for things to be bettered, but, slowly, they were. A group of buildings was finally organized into a new hospital unit called the Buena Vista, and one wonderful day a transport landed thirty-two trained nurses! All the patients who could be moved were transferred to the new unit, but Lora stayed behind with two boys who were dying. She was to stay all night with them—or as long as they lived.

With the relief from strain, she suddenly felt her terrible fatigue. She had been having chills the day before and now, alone with the two dying boys, Lora realized that she too had typhoid fever. Fortunately, one of the doctors looked in to see how things were going, and it was then that Lora collapsed. She did not regain consciousness for three weeks.

It was a long convalescence. Perhaps one of the nicest things about it, aside from the way in which the others spoiled her, was that sometimes her wheel chair was pushed about the grounds of the hospital by one of the boys whom she had nursed.

Three months later she sailed for home, still in a wheel chair. A stay at the nursing home for convalescents in Presidio helped her regain some of her lost strength. And then she headed for Montana and her family.

The family had a new ranch, an orchard this time, and it was near a town which boasted a hospital with a nurse's training school. Lora's hopes for that longed-for diploma rose once more. When she was strong enough she went back to nursing to earn the money for her tuition.

Nurses did not make much money in those days, even the trained ones. And Lora, despite her years of nursing in hospitals, with Associated Charities, private and Army nursing, was still not a trained nurse. She remembered how awed she had been when the nurse sent in to help care for her baby sister charged three dollars for two days!

She knew now that it took a great deal of nursing, much of it twenty-four-hour duty, before the dollars mounted. For months she took on all sorts of cases. Even when she went on her brief vacations, she seemed to be pursued by accidents and sickness with which only she could cope, and her outings were seldom as restful as she had hoped they would be. But she continued to gain in strength, and her small hoard of dollars grew until, at last, she was able to apply to the nursing school for admission.

She trained at a big Catholic hospital, and she was made extremely happy by the decision of the hospital board that she need take only a year and a half of training, since her practical experience had been so extensive and varied.

One of the friendships which she formed at this hospital began unhappily. Isobel, who was also halfway through her training, felt that Lora had been given preferred treatment, and she was quite unfriendly. She certainly did not dream that when she came down with a bad case of diphtheria Lora would be the nurse who would volunteer to be quarantined with her.

Unfortunately the County Detention Hospital was full of cases of smallpox, and so the two girls were sent to a small two-room shack which was used as a pesthouse. It was so dirty when they got there that Lora had to keep Isobel out in the carriage while she cleaned the place.

There were hardly any furnishings. There was no telephone, of course. A wire ran across the fence to the county farm, and there was a bell on the end of it. If Lora wanted anything she pulled on the wire and someone would come as far as the fence to find out what was needed. There was no running water, and the nearest water was from a hydrant fifty feet away. The quarters were far from luxurious!

Isobel was terribly ill. Her fever mounted steadily higher. Lora went on with her scrubbing, trying to make the place as sanitary as possible. It was when she was resting that she saw a man weaving down the road toward the little shack, and she got up to warn him away. He only waved a paper in return, and though she cried out to him that this was a pesthouse, and there was diphtheria there, he came on. When he was close enough to her, Lora saw that he was very ill. He, too, had diphtheria. So now she had two patients.

There were, however, only two beds, so Lora took a mattress from the tent the county farm people sent her, and she slept on the floor. She had hardly settled herself when a man started to climb in the window.

"Don't come in here!" Lora yelled. "This is a pesthouse!" But he swung his legs over the sill and said, "That's why I'm here." He was Isobel's brother Al, and he insisted on staying to help Lora with her two delirious patients. He had had a shot of serum before he came and had found a shack just over the hill in which to camp. He told her he would come in every night to take over so that she could get some rest, and that is exactly what he did until his sister was well again.

From the time of her illness, Isobel not only lost all resentment toward Lora but even became dependent upon her, for she was left with a grave thyroid condition which kept her a semi-invalid. She was some years younger than Lora and called her "Ma." Lora, in her turn, felt protective toward this young woman whose life she had saved, and she always tried to keep an eye on her to see that she didn't overdo.

On the night of her graduation from the nursing school, there was a terrible storm. A doctor

whom Lora admired very much gave them their diplomas and made a little speech. In it he said, "The most thrilling thing in life is Struggle." Lora fastened upon those words, for they seemed to be meant especially for her. Surely few women had had such a struggle as she had had to reach her goal of being a trained nurse! She received her diploma when she was thirty-one years old. And she sensed that the struggle was not over for her. All her life she would have to work against odds, she knew, yet she welcomed them, for she was a born fighter, as all good nurses are.

There were to be many hard places ahead. Not long after graduation, she was sent up into the Blackfoot Hills to nurse a young man who had typhoid fever. There was an epidemic in the area, and little aid could be counted on from the neighbors. On the isolated ranch there were only the rancher and his wife, and their son who was so desperately ill. They had lost their other four children, and all their hopes were centered now upon the sick young man.

But Eddie did not want to live. The girl he was in love with had run away with another man, and he had lost all interest in life. Now Lora knew that she would have a real fight on her hands, for anyone as sick as he, and who was over-burdened with an inner despair, was a difficult case indeed.

She nursed him devotedly for more than three months. The boy's parents did everything that they could to help, the doctor advised over the telephone, the forest ranger dropped in to do what he could, a trapper who had once been a doctor came to spell her in her fatiguing duty. But every-thing failed, and the boy died. She had lost this long battle with death, and Lora was exhausted. But she knew that she had put up a good fight; that no one could have done more than she.

There were other, happier experiences to com-pensate for those that were tragic. One time she was called to a farm to care for a woman who was expecting her third child, and she drove up to the farmhouse just in time to deliver it—without the doctor. That was a thrill that she never forgot, although, as she said in her book, *No Time for Tears,* "My knee joints felt as though they were mere jelly all the rest of the day."

There were amusing experiences, too, and Lora was always able to see the funny side of a situation, even when it was one that others would have found annoying. When she nursed a wealthy woman (who didn't have much the matter with her) and the patient decided Lora should do a large hamper of linen laundry to earn her fee, Lora got the better of her by saying that she would do the laundry if the woman would use the poorly paid laundress as nurse. Then she proceeded to give a lot of complex instructions to the laundress, and the frightened patient changed her mind.

For some time, now, she had been living in Seattle, where she had bought a house. She had her family with her much of the time. And Isobel, too, of course. Isobel's brother had long since gone to Alberta, in Canada, where he was homesteading with his friend Jock, and one of the dreams Lora and Isobel had always had was to visit the boys some day. They had to wait until a railroad had been built, but as soon as it was finished, they were on their way.

Al and his partner Jock had two cabins built above a small spring-fed lake, with barns and sheds and stables. Lora was right at home. It was pioneering all over again, and she felt as if she were back in her childhood. She had never lost her love of wide vistas, and the Canadian bush appealed to her.

Neighbors were few and far between, but there were several get-togethers. The happiest of all was the Christmas party which was held at the homestead. Before they left home, Lora and Isobel had invited their friends to make contributions for just such a party, and they brought tree trimmings and gifts for children and grownups, as well as a portable phonograph and records.

It was a wonderful party. Many of the children had never seen a tinseled tree, or gay gift wrappings. When it was over, those who lived nearby went home, but the others bedded down upon the floor of the cabins on straw ticks and blankets.

Lora went back to Seattle and her nursing work after this interlude, and she gave many years of happy service to the ill. She was a charter member of the Nurses' Association of the Northwest. She never forgot what she had heard on her stormy commencement night, "The most thrilling thing in life is Struggle."

She knew it now; knew that it was struggle which had made her childhood so memorable; knew that it was the struggle to obtain her nurse's training which had made it so worthwhile. She realized, too, that although sometimes a nurse lost the battle with death, it was that struggle to save which mattered and which was, in the end, a kind of winning.

Whitman
CLASSICS

Five Little Peppers Midway

Freckles

Wild Animals I Have Known

Rebecca of Sunnybrook
    Farm

Alice in Wonderland

Mrs. Wiggs of the
    Cabbage Patch

Fifty Famous Fairy Tales

Rose in Bloom

Eight Cousins

Little Women

Little Men

Five Little Peppers and
    How They Grew

Robinson Crusoe

Treasure Island

Heidi

The Call of the Wild

Tom Sawyer

Beautiful Joe

Adventures of Sherlock Holmes

Here are some of the best-loved stories of all time.
Delightful ... intriguing ... never-to-be-forgotten
tales that you will read again and again. Start
your own home library of WHITMAN CLASSICS
so that you'll always have exciting books at your
finger tips.

Whitman

REG. U.S. PAT. OFF.

Whitman ADVENTURE and MYSTERY Books